NEW ESSAYS ON MOBY-DICK

★ The American Novel ★

GENERAL EDITOR

Emory Elliott, Princeton University

Other books in the series:
New Essays on The Scarlet Letter
New Essays on The Great Gatsby
New Essays on Adventures of Huckleberry Finn
New Essays on Uncle Tom's Cabin
New Essays on The Red Badge of Courage

Forthcoming:
New Essays on Chopin's The Awakening (ed. Wendy Martin)
New Essays on Ellison's Invisible Man (ed. Robert O'Meally)
New Essays on Light in August (ed. Michael Millgate)
New Essays on The Sun Also Rises (ed. Linda Wagner)
New Essays on James's The American (ed. Martha Banta)

New Essays on
Moby-Dick

Edited by

Richard H. Brodhead

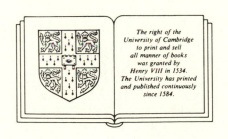

The right of the
University of Cambridge
to print and sell
all manner of books
was granted by
Henry VIII in 1534.
The University has printed
and published continuously
since 1584.

CAMBRIDGE UNIVERSITY PRESS

Cambridge

London   New York   New Rochelle

Melbourne   Sydney

Published by the Press Syndicate of the University of Cambridge
The Pitt Building, Trumpington Street, Cambridge CB2 1RP
32 East 57th Street, New York, NY 10022, USA
10 Stamford Road, Oakleigh, Melbourne 3166, Australia

First published 1986

Printed in the United States of America

Library of Congress Cataloging-in-Publication Data
New essays on Moby-Dick.
(The American novel)
Bibliography: p.
1. Melville, Herman, 1819–1891.   Moby Dick.
I. Brodhead, Richard H., 1947–   . II. Series.
PS2384.M62N48   1986   813'.3   86-9738

British Library Cataloguing in Publication Data
New essays on Moby-Dick.–(The American novel)
1. Melville, Herman. Moby Dick
I. Brodhead, Richard H. II. Series
818'.3   PS2384.M62

ISBN 0 521 30205 6 hard covers
ISBN 0 521 31788 6 paperback

Contents

Contents

Series Editor's Preface

In literary criticism the last twenty-five years have been particularly fruitful. Since the rise of the New Criticism in the 1950s, which focused attention of critics and readers upon the text itself – apart from history, biography, and society – there has emerged a wide variety of critical methods which have brought to literary works a rich diversity of perspectives: social, historical, political, psychological, economic, ideological, and philosophical. While attention to the text itself, as taught by the New Critics, remains at the core of contemporary interpretation, the widely shared assumption that works of art generate many different kinds of interpretation has opened up possibilities for new readings and new meanings.

Before this critical revolution, many American novels had come to be taken for granted by earlier generations of readers as having an established set of recognized interpretations. There was a sense among many students that the canon was established and that the larger thematic and interpretative issues had been decided. The task of the new reader was to examine the ways in which elements such as structure, style, and imagery contributed to each novel's acknowledged purpose. But recent criticism has brought these old assumptions into question and has thereby generated a wide variety of original, and often quite surprising, interpretations of the classics, as well as of rediscovered novels such as Kate Chopin's *The Awakening*, which has only recently entered the canon of works that scholars and critics study and that teachers assign their students.

The aim of The American Novel Series is to provide students of American literature and culture with introductory critical guides to

American novels now widely read and studied. Each volume is devoted to a single novel and begins with an introduction by the volume editor, a distinguished authority on the text. The introduction presents details of the novel's composition, publication history, and contemporary reception, as well as a survey of the major critical trends and readings from first publication to the present. This overview is followed by four or five original essays, specifically commissioned from senior scholars of established reputation and from outstanding younger critics. Each essay presents a distinct point of view, and together they constitute a forum of interpretative methods and of the best contemporary ideas on each text.

It is our hope that these volumes will convey the vitality of current critical work in American literature, generate new insights and excitement for students of the American novel, and inspire new respect for and new perspectives upon these major literary texts.

Emory Elliott
Princeton University

Trying All Things: An Introduction to *Moby-Dick*

RICHARD H. BRODHEAD

1

HERMAN Melville has been acknowledged, in our time if not in his own, as one of American literature's greatest authors. Our time has also seen *Moby-Dick* — probably more than any other American novel — enshrined in the ranks of literature's ultimate achievements. But we are in danger of missing the special quality of Melville as a writer and of *Moby-Dick* as an act of writing if we think of them as sitting peacefully inside such sedate categories. If *Moby-Dick* is a classic, it is so very much on its own terms. What sets it apart is not really its whaling subject, and not even its famous depths of symbolic meaning, so much as the stand it takes toward literature itself — its quite peculiar attitude, registered on every page, toward what literature is and can be, and toward what it can attempt as a work of literary making.

Moby-Dick's great hero gives one measure of what I mean. Melville's ravaged and fanatic captain, so overscaled in his energies and so restricted in his range of interests, is in one sense a variant on a classic American type. Monomania, a rare personality disorder in everyday life, has something of the status of a normal state of selfhood in American fiction. From Charles Brockden Brown's compulsive ventriloquist to Hawthorne's questers after knowledge and Poe's fetishists of tooth and eye to the rigidified regional obsessives of Sarah Orne Jewett and Sherwood Anderson, Faulkner's tracers of unalterable designs, and Flannery O'Connor's involuntary baptisers and tattoo seekers, American fiction's most distinctive fantasies have commonly featured the figure of the monomaniac, the self mastered by a single motive and so restricted to a single move or goal. Captain Ahab is, of course, the classic embodiment of this figure. But what is characteristic of Melville is that when he seizes on this common literary property, he instantly endows it with the power and presence of the full-fledged heroic self. He equips his obsessive with the hero's unforgettably distinguishing name – *"he's Ahab,* boy" (Chap. 16), Captain Peleg rightly underlines. He equips him with the hero's special linguistic register – the gorgeously musical metaphorical language Ahab seems less to speak than to declaim or sing. He equips him with the hero's magnanimity, his outsized capacities to will, do, feel, and suffer: Ahab wills not as we will but as a locomotive drives along a track; Ahab sobs not as we sob but with the superior woe of "a heart-stricken moose" (Chap. 36). And he equips him with the hero's memorable *story* or adventure – in this case, to hunt and to be destroyed by hunting the great white whale.

Captain Ahab is one of the few American contributions to that handful of resonant names – like Hamlet, or Lear, or Oedipus, or Faust – that seem to sum up some fact of human potential and to bare the contours of some exemplary human fate. If Ahab has joined this company, it is because Melville *imagines* him heroically: grasps and realizes him within a heroic conception of the self. This unattenuated heroism is an impressive feature of *Moby-Dick* as a finished book. But it also bespeaks its distinctive spirit, the enabling literary attitude in which the book is attempted. When the author of *Moby-Dick* thinks of literature, his revival of the heroic mode reminds us, he associates it scarcely at all with the literary forms most active in his own time. Instead he drives literature back to its most primal and potent forms: identifies it with epic, quest narrative, and heroic tragedy, the forms of its most ancient and enduring achievements. And as he exhumes the idea of these forms, he also insists that they are still practicable now. He reads heroic literature in one way as a set of great achievements but in another as a set of imaginative *acts,* acts he asserts his right to do again in making a work of his own.

Part of what makes *Moby-Dick* stand out, in the company of literary classics, is its quality of raw literary presumptuousness – its cheeky confidence that nothing great has ever been done that it

2

can't at least try to do again. And it is a correlative of this presumptuousness that although *Moby-Dick* lays claim to everything
great literature has achieved, it also refuses to acknowledge traditional literature's systems of restraint. The traditional high literary
forms — tragedy and epic, most notably — observe fairly strict
literary protocols. They do things in certain ways and not in others. Melville knows this; and in his zeal to reclaim what he thinks
of as the genres of greatness, he can follow their programs quite
carefully, for two or three chapters at a time. But Melville refuses
to accept that part of the traditional compact that says that, while
writing one kind of work, one must give up the will to be writing
another. The obvious proof is that although the rudiments of a
Shakespearean heroic tragedy can be spotted in *Moby-Dick*, they
share textual space with masses of material that lie quite outside
that tragedy. The book in which we learn something great about
the internal contradictions of unqualified will is also the book in
which we learn all sorts of little things about whales and their
habits — how they breathe, for instance (a constant number of
surface breaths in a fixed interval); or how they see (with two
nonoverlapping visual fields and a blind spot to the front); or how
they mate [*"more hominum"* (Chap. 87)]. Similarly, the book that,
in one of its aspects, thrusts irreversibly forward toward its hero's
appointed end is also the book that traces, much more mean-
deringly, the sequence of tasks needed to put up a killed whale's
blubber in the form of processed oil.

The so-called cetological center of *Moby-Dick*, that mass of chapters story lovers love to skip, in fact could make a vigorous book in
its own right. Properly separated and slightly amplified, these
chapters could form a great work of American commodity history.
They do for whale oil lighting what Richard Henry Dana's *Two
Years Before the Mast* does for the cattle hides that become our
shoes, or what Frank Norris's *The Octopus* and *The Pit* do for the
wheat that becomes our daily bread: They bring back to visibility,
behind some product so familiar as to be a precondition for everyday life, the forgotton process by which it has been first wrenched
out of natural life, then worked or manufactured into a marketable
good. (We will continue to lack our world's full equivalent for

Moby-Dick until we have a great novel of the oil or nuclear power industry, a novel that will bring us knowledge of how the light we read it by is made.)[1]

But it is the nature of *Moby-Dick* that this commodity narrative is not given us as a book by itself, any more than Melville's quest tragedy is. Instead *Moby-Dick* delights in being heterogeneous – a work of mixed and discordant kinds, amalgamating into itself every form of writing (so it would seem) that strikes its fancy. Formally, *Moby-Dick* is always becoming something else, always deciding what kind of book it will be next; and its hectic shape shiftings bespeak, again, the peculiar *idea* of literature that governs this work. The book that will not pass up the chance also to do an Elizabethan soliloquy, and also a Calvinist sermon, and also a parody of a legal brief, and also an experimental operatic ensemble number (as in "Midnight, Forecastle") is a work strong in the sense of the whole, unfractioned power of literary utterance – a work that glories in the recognition, behind the separate generic forms that define and constrain it, of what *all* writing can express or do. Accordingly, its idea of the proper way of being literary is not to fill out the outline of some predetermined literary kind but rather to do everything at once: to embrace and display, in an exuberance of renewed invention, the full form of writing's expressive potential.

Moby-Dick's unwillingness to do one literary thing at the expense of another is part of what keeps it from pursuing its story straightforwardly. But another pressure keeps disrupting it too: the pressure of passionate philosophical surmise. As *Moby-Dick* describes it, the most elemental human passion is not love, or ambition, or acquisitiveness, but something more like anxiety – anxiety, specifically, about the ground of our being, an anxiety that drives us, whatever our immediate situation, to keep worrying the question how the world is framed and governed. Ahab is the most obvious victim of this passion. Ahab's disease is that he can't keep from extrapolating from local experiences to their cosmological implications – can't see elemental force, as in "The Candles," without thinking a world ruled by gods of force; can't see the insane Pip, as in "The Log and Line," without seeing too the "creative libertines" (Chap. 125) who allow such humanly intolerable sights.

4

But the passion Ahab feels so unqualifiedly is lived, at different levels of intensity, by all of Melville's characters. (Stubb's "I wonder, Flask, whether the world is anchored anywhere" [Chap. 121] is a typical passing remark in this cosmologically anxious book.) And this same passion informs the book itself as an act of thought. The energies of literary composition are so interfused with the energies of philosophical surmise in *Moby-Dick* that every stray particular that enters the book is in immediate danger of being seized on and pressed to yield a model of the world. Whale-lines are functional tools, made of certain materials in certain thicknesses, but only until they get caught in the updraft of cosmological generalization: "But why say more? All men live enveloped in whale-lines" (Chap. 60). Sharks are fierce scavengers, fascinating wonders of natural ravenousness, but they too get pressed to yield a statement about the world's creator: "de god wat made shark must be one dam Injin" (Chap. 66).

Moby-Dick's always renewed thrust toward ultimate statement gives it its distinctive rhythm as a meditation in prose. It also produces what must be the most remarkable achievement in the book: the way *Moby-Dick* manages, not once but over and over, to project a vision of the world's essential constitution, and not vaguely but with sustained precision of articulated detail. "The Chapel" thus lets us see – where else did we ever grasp this possibility so concretely? – a world peopled with the dead, filled with the void of the nonexistent. "The Grand Armada" lets us see a world centered in generative and nurturing love, in its *Paradiso* vision of nursing mother whales; "The Castaway" lets us see a world formed through speechless, unmindful natural process; and so on. These acts of cosmic knowing are among the most distinctive literary accomplishments of *Moby-Dick*, and they remind us of something else Melville takes the literary to mean. For as *Moby-Dick* presumes to practice it, literature is simply not a secular art. First and last things, the state of the world and our place in it, are not the province of some other cultural system called religion, *Moby-Dick* asserts. They are instead literature's province, questions literature is empowered to address and explore. Moreover, Melville presumes that literature has the power not just to retell religious truth already arrived at but to deliver religion's realm *to* knowledge, to grasp and speak it into comprehensible form – as "The Whiteness of the Whale," to give one last example, literally *develops* the idea of a cosmic blankness outside the sphere of mind, through the churnings of its prose.

Melville's activation of literature as an art claiming these great powers gives *Moby-Dick* its peculiar form of seriousness. Like scripture or vision narrative or wisdom writing – genres that it also draws into itself – *Moby-Dick* makes the heightened claim on our attention not that good writing does, but of speech that engages the ultimate dimensions of our existence. But if *Moby-Dick* reaches beyond the usual registers of literary expression, this leads to no devaluation of writing, but to intensified care for writing as such. More persistently than anything else – more persistently than it is heroic, or philosophic, or whatever – *Moby-Dick* is a book in love with language. It is so in love with the sound of words that it savors their spoken heft as it writes them. It is so in love with the infinitude of language that it always wants to use more of it, to heap high all the actual or conceivable words that any textual space will support. ("He tasks me; he heaps me" [Chap. 36] is a *Moby-Dick* locution; so is "devoured, chewed up, crunched" [Chap. 16], or "infixed, unrelenting fangs" [Chap. 41], or "heathenish, sharked waters and . . . unrecorded, javelin islands" [Chap. 24].) But it is peculiarly the case with *Moby-Dick* that its addiction to the act of putting things in words, or what we could call its sheer indulgence in language, serves as the means by which it drives its insights into knowledge. *Moby-Dick* loves to amplify. Having half-said something, its urge is always to stop and say it again. And this process of rhetorical elaboration is, on page after page, how it finally manages to say what at first eluded its grasp. If we end up with some idea of the spiritual torments that fuel Ahab's quest for revenge, it is because Melville keeps naming what exasperates Ahab (I break the passage to mark its iterations):

> All that most maddens and torments;
> all that stirs up the lees of things;
> all truth with malice in it;
> all that cracks the sinews and cakes the brain;

6

all the subtle demonisms of life and thought;
all evil, to crazy Ahab, was visibly personified, and made
practically assailable in Moby Dick. (Chap. 41)

If we finally begin to understand the dreadful blankness Ishmael
associates with the white whale's whiteness, it is because he keeps
renewing his surmise, more and more ingeniously naming the
nothing he addresses:

Is it that by its indefiniteness it shadows forth the heartless voids
and immensities of the universe, and thus stabs us from behind with
the thought of annihilation, when beholding the white depths of
the milky way?
Or is it, that as in essence whiteness is not so much a color as the
visible absence of color, and at the same time the concrete of all
colors;
is it for these reasons that there is such a dumb blankness, full of
meaning, in a wide landscape of snows – a colorless, all-color of
atheism from which we shrink? (Chap. 42)

If we come more fully to realize the blind, unmindful destructiveness embodied in the beautifully deadly sea, it is because
Melville's repetitions drive through our usual obliviousness:

But though, to landsmen in general, the native inhabitants of the
seas have ever been regarded with emotions unspeakably unsocial
and repelling;
though we know the sea to be everlasting terra incognita, so that
Columbus sailed over numberless unknown worlds to discover his
superficial western one;
though, by vast odds, the most terrific of all mortal disasters have
immemorially and indiscriminately befallen tens and hundreds of
thousands of those who have gone upon the waters;
though but a moment's consideration will teach, that however
much baby man may brag of his science and skill, and however
much, in a flattering future, that science and skill may augment; yet
for ever and for ever, to the crack of doom, the sea will insult and
murder him, and pulverize the stateliest, stiffest frigate he can
make;
nevertheless, by the continual repetition of these very impres-

sions, man has lost that sense of the full awfulness of the sea which aboriginally belongs to it. (Chap. 58)

If we begin to grasp the mixed and quite elusive motives that drive Ishmael to that sea in the first place, it is because he does not just name his reasons, but rhetorically elaborates them:

> Whenever I find myself growing grim about the mouth;
> whenever it is a damp, drizzly November in my soul;
> whenever I find myself involuntarily pausing before coffin ware-
> houses, and bringing up the rear of every funeral I meet;
> and especially whenever my hypos get such an upper hand of me,
> that it requires a strong moral principle to prevent me from deliber-
> ately stepping into the street, and methodically knocking people's
> hats off –
> then, I account it high time to get to sea as soon as I can. (Chap.
> 1)

I have been claiming that *Moby-Dick*'s uniqueness as a work of literature lies in the pressure it puts *on* literature. My argument has been that *Moby-Dick* does not accept literature as an already de-fined notion, but searches the idea of it to its roots; that it not only *is* literature in some familiar sense, therefore, but dramatically reexposes literature's radical powers. Melville's revival of liter-ature's powers of heroic imagination is part of this demonstration. So is his revival of fiction as a source of cosmological knowledge. But if we want to locate the most fundamental fact of literature that *Moby-Dick* displays, we need to look to the life of its language. *Moby-Dick* is, no more and no less than any literary work, a con-trivance of language. Like all the other members of this category, it is, like the song of Wallace Stevens's singing girl at Key West, "uttered word by word." But *Moby-Dick*'s special marks, as a con-trivance of words, are, first, that it displays the resources of lan-guage so splendidly, and second, that it makes its act of imagina-tive speaking be its agent of discovery, the very medium of its cognition. As such, *Moby-Dick* reminds us of what we know in a sense but usually fail to appreciate: that literature is not only cre-ated *in* words but creates *through* its words; that if it gives us the world to apprehend anew, it does not do so apart from its lan-guage, but through its vital working of the medium of words.

8

2

When Ishmael sets out to track the sources of Ahab's obsession, he keeps feeling his way forward from one kind of explanation to another. And as he completes what would seem to be the climax of his explanation, he takes care to remember that no explanation can be fully sufficient to its object: "This is much; yet Ahab's larger, darker, deeper part remains unhinted" (Chap. 41). I want to say a few words here about the sources of *Moby-Dick*'s creation. But I do so cautioned that such an account will be useful only if it is flexible, and if it does not presume to be the whole of the truth.

The most provocative recent criticism of Melville has reminded us that *Moby-Dick*, although it makes little reference to the contemporary social world, is in fact steeped in the concerns of mid-nineteenth-century American culture. Michael Paul Rogin's *Subversive Genealogy: The Politics and Art of Herman Melville* reminds us that the crisis of artistic creation that produced *Moby-Dick* coincided exactly with the national political crisis that helped bare the inevitability of civil war – the crisis induced by the Mexican War of 1848, the grand gesture of American expansionism, which in the act of adding new land to the American nation brought its old divisions between slave state and free state back to explosive life. Rogin's book helps us to recognize that Ahab, literature's classic figure of ego assertion brought to the pitch of an unswervable mission – "The path to my fixed purpose is laid with iron rails, whereon my soul is grooved to run" (Chap. 37) – expresses in literary form the same energies that are expressed politically in American expansionism. Rogin also helps us to suspect that Ahab's tragedy might be read, on one level, as a meditation on the disastrous consequences that the raw expansionist drive might unleash. Ann Douglas's *The Feminization of American Culture* reminds us that the culture Rogin describes as polarized over sectional interests was also going through a crisis of gender reorganization, a sharpening of the separation between the public and economically productive sphere of men and the private sphere of home, family, and culture reserved for women. *Moby-Dick* is a novel so outrageously masculine that we scarcely allow ourselves to do justice to the full scope of its masculinism. It is a masculine

9

book in the obvious sense that it is all about men and mens' activities. (The feminine sphere as the nineteenth century described it – the sphere of piety, home, family love and nurture, and general sociability – is the missing element in a novel otherwise so inclusive.) But it is masculine too in its deepest dramatic fantasies: What is the hunt for the enormous sperm whale Moby Dick if not a quest for absolute potency, a quest in which the aggressive assertion of masculine strength calls up a fantastically enlarged version of that strength as its imagined nemesis? Douglas's account of history helps us see both the outrageous masculineness of Melville's imagining and also that this deeply personal feature of his imagining has a cultural source – derives from, even as it revolts against, the general social redivision of gender prerogatives taking place in Melville's time.[2]

Accounts like Rogin's and Douglas's are immensely helpful in recovering lost dimensions of *Moby-Dick*'s cultural origins. But taking them together is useful too – not least because it reminds us that the culture *Moby-Dick* comes out of is organized in not one but many ways, each of which this book could help us more actively understand. Accordingly, we might ask, what is *Moby-Dick?* A fantasia on themes of expansionism and masculinity, surely, but also a great exercise in declamatory rhetoric. And in its rhetorical display, *Moby-Dick* might remind us that American culture of the 1840s and 1850s is also a profoundly rhetorical culture – a culture whose dominant verbal form is still the spoken word, and especially the spoken word embellished into self-conscious oratory. (The prose style of *Moby-Dick* would seem less strange to us if we read it aloud alongside such contemporaneous forms as the sermon, the political oration, theatrical rant, or the school declamation piece.) Or we might start another investigation by asking: What is *Moby-Dick?* A feast of periodic rhetoric, but also a work of religious reflection and speculation. In this capacity, the book gives us an indication of the fact that American culture of the mid-nineteenth century is also a not yet secularized culture, a culture in which the world of literature (as of politics) is still directly open to religion's energies, idioms, and concerns. (*Uncle Tom's Cabin*, in so many ways the photographic negative of *Moby-Dick*, shares this feature with its exact contemporary: It is literary in a sense that joins, not separates, literature's and oratory's and religion's cultural spheres.)

Moby-Dick has been treated so much as the idiosyncratic work of an individual genius that any way we can find to recover its larger cultural sources is bound to seem especially valuable. Nevertheless, at some point an account of this book's origins has to acknowledge that it also derives from circumstances more immediately personal, some of which bear retelling here. Melville was born, in 1819, to a family prominent on both parents' sides. This family seemed to be renovating the foundations of its social position through Melville's father's business ventures. But this adventurous merchant-entrepreneur failed, then died, in Melville's early teens, leaving a family trained for prosperity to depend on the kindness of relatives. This wrenching dislocation had consequences for Melville's whole life attitude that we would be hard pressed to mark the limit of. They reveal themselves, very obviously, in his fourth book, *Redburn,* with its touchiness about social status and its anxiety to reassert a threatened gentility. ("The Sailor Boy Confessions of the Son-of-a-Gentleman," this book's subtitle reads in part.) But we might wonder whether Melville's experience of disentitlement is not expressed even more powerfully in *Moby-Dick:* in the sense of existential impairment that Ahab would avenge himself for, or in the general attitude of dispossession that finds its biblical name in Ishmael.

Whatever we might say that it produced in the long run, the short-term consequences his father's failure had for Melville are clear enough. To keep from draining his family's damaged fortunes, he tried out for a variety of jobs that required little investment of resources. He became a clerk; later he became a schoolteacher; later still, he signed on as a sailor.

Any biography will lay out the sequence of merchant, whaling, and naval vessels that Melville enlisted on (and deserted from) between his twentieth and twenty-fifth years. Here it might only be noted that the principal meaning of these years for Melville's writing life is that his apprenticeship for literature was emphatically not served *in* literature. The author of *Moby-Dick* is the most bookish of authors. But he could scarcely feel so free to shuffle high and low or literary and nonliterary sources together — let alone to feel that *he* could do what he admired in great authors – if his sense of literature was not largely the product of idiosyncratic enthusiasms. His sense of his right to invent literature – his freedom from indoctrination into literature as a formalized cultural institution – is one thing Melville owes to his nonliterary training. Another is also easy to name. If *Moby-Dick* is the most bookish, and possibly even the most mental or abstract, of nineteenth-century novels, it is essential to its success that its abstractions never pull entirely loose from the sharp particulars of the whaler's life – from its information about boats and whales; but even more, from the visceral knowledge of how men and whales look, feel, and behave in the violence of their encounter. If Melville had this knowledge to draw on, it is because he had nonliterary experience: experience of the tough, exposed world of the sailor's work.

When Melville came home at the age of twenty-five, he quickly found that his sailor's years were a stock he could trade on. In 1845 he wrote an account of the adventures he had when he jumped ship in the Marquesas Islands, which, published as *Typee*, had an instant success. By this act the former clerk, teacher, and sailor – possibly without much more forethought or prior dedication than had gone into those jobs – found another career open up for him, as the writer of his colorful experiences.

Hereafter Melville's plan seems to have been simply to settle into this unexpectedly comfortable position. In 1846 and 1847 he set about in brisk, businesslike fashion to produce more versions of the ware he had found a market for. ("Calculated for popular reading, or for none at all"[3] is Melville's literary motto at this time.) On the basis of his restored prospects he also settled down, marrying and setting up a new family establishment. But just at this point, something happened to Melville's new work. Writing, first used to record adventures already experienced, suddenly became a source of adventure its own right. In the middle of his third Polynesian travel book, with a display of the nerve that hereafter became one of his chief authorial marks, Melville threw over his initial plan and, without bothering to remove its traces, changed his book into something else – first an allegorical quest-romance, then a kind of philosophical-satirical symposium, then something not unlike a journal: a thinking book, a book in which to write

12

down unorganized thoughts as they occur, to see what they could be developed into.

In composing this third work, *Mardi*, in 1848 and 1849, Melville reinvented himself as an experimental author. He devised here the experimental form in which his most ambitious work would be written: that sprung narrative, open to improvisation and accommodating the play of rival designs, of which *Moby-Dick* is the great example. Equally important, Melville also worked out here a literary attitude that justified such formal innovations. The act of writing, Melville here came to believe, could have more interesting aims than to tell stories or rehearse experiences. More energetically pursued, writing could be a means of self-development. Giving oneself up to writing, obeying no advance plan except to say as vigorously as one can whatever occurs to one, makes writing, *Mardi* suggests, a thought-*creating* act: a means to drive latent thought forward to articulation, a way to realize the potential of one's mind. In this novel's self-justifying words: "When Lombardo set about his work, he knew not what it would become. He did not build himself in with plans; he wrote right on; and so doing, got deeper and deeper into himself."[4]

By the time he had finished *Mardi*, we can see retroactively, Melville had devised the structural prototype for *Moby-Dick*. But one of the most curious facts of Melville's career is that it was only after he completed this rather zany experiment that he became subject to the deep urgencies this structure would eventually be called to bear the weight of. One of the notable novelties of *Mardi* is that the great Polynesian traveler has suddenly become a great reader. This book's author has digested (or, as is more Melville's way, half-digested) a library of rather heterogeneous texts, from Rabelais to Seneca and Shaftesbury to the fantasist de la Motte Fouqué. And already here, Melville shows his great characteristic as a reader – namely, that instead of patiently subordinating himself to the works he reads, he prefers to catch their idea on the fly, then try it in writing of his own. But it was really only after the *Mardi* experiment that Melville discovered literature as a kingdom of greatness. His letters and essays of 1849 and 1850 show him responding, with mounting waves of rapturous enthusiasm, to the row of great authors he had only now discovered. "Dolt & ass that

I am I have lived more than 29 years, & until a few days ago, never made close acquaintance with the divine William. Ah, he's full of sermons-on-the-mount, and gentle, aye, almost as Jesus,"[5] he wrote of Shakespeare in 1849. Hawthorne, whom he first read in the summer of 1850, brought him the even more electrifying sense that literature's "Shiloh, or 'Master Genius' '"[6] need be no ancient author but could be reborn here and now. It is at this time that Melville, already a bookmonger, became so receptive to what literature's powerful forms can do. And it is here that this writer, for four years an author of sorts, began fiercely to aspire to be one of literature's giants and to do its great work anew.

At the same time that this realm opened up to him, Melville began to break through into another world with its own elating opportunities and fierce ambitions: the world of what *Moby-Dick* calls "deep, earnest thinking" (Chap. 23). The Melville of *Mardi* differs from his earlier self in his itch to take up questions like the compatibility of fate and free will or the authority of scripture and reason. But these potentially great questions are little more than mental puzzles to the author of this book. It is after *Mardi* that metaphysical issues come to have pressing, even tormenting personal reality for Melville. In 1856 Nathaniel Hawthorne described a Melville every reader will recognize:

> Melville, as he always does, began to reason of Providence and futurity, and of everything that lies beyond human ken, and informed me that he had "pretty much made up his mind to be annihilated"; but still he does not seem to rest in that anticipation; and, I think, will never rest until he gets hold of a definite belief. It is strange how he persists – and has persisted ever since I knew him, and probably long before – in wandering to-and-fro over these deserts, as dismal and monotonous as the sand hills amid which we were sitting. He can neither believe, nor be comfortable in his disbelief; and he is too honest and courageous not to try to do one or the other.[7]

The written record suggests that the demon of metaphysical speculation seized on Melville around 1850. This is when Mrs. Hawthorne described Melville as a hyperintense gentleman caller, speaking "his innermost about GOD, the Devil & Life if so be he can get at the Truth."[8] His letters, full of ease and generous enthusiasms before, become at this time grimly driven, unable to leave the question of the anchoring of our world or the quest for an independent position toward first things.

The Melville of 1850 knew he was in crisis. This crisis was in the fullest sense a crisis of faith: a state in which the question of how the world is held together had wrenched itself violently open. But this crisis was also in no trivial sense a literary crisis – not just because Melville also felt tempted and burdened by great literary ambitions, but because he looked to literature as the place where that crisis of cosmology could be addressed. As he became tasked and heaped by his own inscrutable things, Melville increasingly identified literature as a vehicle of revelation. In his 1850 essay "Hawthorne and His Mosses," he calls great literature's verbal gestures "probings at the very axis of reality." Accordingly, he regards literature not as an art form merely but as potentially reality *disclosing:* a "great Art of Telling the Truth."[9]

What Melville did, when he set about creating *Moby-Dick,* was to choose to face and work through this compound crisis by means of his writing. Having, in the wake of *Mardi,* at least temporarily renounced his experimental ambitions, Melville turned two more chapters of his sailor years into books the following year. In the spring and summer of 1850, apparently continuing this plan of action, he began a book based on the last unexploited portion of his early adventures: his life in the sperm whale fishery. But here again he changed his plan, as he emboldened himself to take greater risks. The new project he set himself, sometime later that year, was to use the matter of whaling as a matrix in which to work out his newfound ambitions: to unfold his mind through the play of composition; to do the work of a literary genius; and if not to solve, then at least to struggle to hold open, the question of the founding of this world. Everything we know about Melville in the year he spent composing *Moby-Dick* shows a writer charged, even to excess, with expressive energies: "I can't stop yet," his letters of this time keep saying. Everything we know suggests a writer in the strictest sense absorbed in his work: By at least one account, Melville stopped coming out of his writing room even for food while finishing *The Whale.*[10] This biographical testimony tells us on what terms *Moby-Dick* was written. It is the work of a writer for whom writing has become an arena of intense speculative adventure; the work of a writer whose deepest life concerns are being engaged *through* the writer's act.

3

With Melville, writing is always strongly allied with ongoing growth and change of mind. So it is not surprising that, after *Moby-Dick*, he quickly went on to do other kinds of work – including work that makes quite other assumptions about literature's nature and power. But it seems clear that, when he finished this book, Melville thought of it as a great effort completed. And we know that he hungered to have it recognized. When Hawthorne wrote him to acknowledge *Moby-Dick*'s achievement, Melville responded with unparalleled elation. His letters elsewhere show him depressed by the fear that the book would not be recognized as his major work. While finishing *Moby-Dick* he wrote Hawthorne:

> What "reputation" H.M. has is horrible. Think of it! To go down to posterity is bad enough, any way; but to go down as a "man who lived among the cannibals"! When I speak of posterity, in reference to myself, I only mean the babies who will probably be born in the moment immediately ensuing upon my giving up the ghost. I shall go down to some of them, in all likelihood. "Typee" will be given them, perhaps, with their gingerbread."[11]

Melville was largely right that his contemporaries would not rise to the challenge of *Moby-Dick*. When the book was published – in October 1851 (under the title *The Whale*) in England, and in November 1851 in America – its reviews were by no means all negative or undiscerning. At a time when *Moby-Dick* was still innocent of any critical reputation, one reviewer had the penetration to call it "a prose Epic on Whaling," and another to see that it was "not a mere tale of adventures, but a whole philosophy of life."[12] But for every reviewer who admired Melville's work there was another unwilling to enter into the spirit of his experiment. *Moby-Dick*, proof to one reader that Melville was a man of genius, was proof to another that he was a literary "incorrigible," a writer unwilling or unable to obey the rules of his art. For readers of this persuasion, the unusual demands Melville makes on literature

16

were the very things that rendered *Moby-Dick* unacceptable. The book's heterogeneity, its inclusion of plural and competing kinds of literature, was recognized, but as a fault, by the reviewer who called it "an ill-compounded mixture of romance and matter-of-fact." Its hyperactivity of style was noted, but as a flaw, by the reviewer who termed its language "maniacal." And its philosophical reach and ardent speculative energy were grasped, but as a source of pain, not wonder, by the reviewer who condemned its "piratical running down of creeds and opinions."[13]

Moby-Dick had a mixed critical reception, but its situation among general readers was worse than its reviews suggest. The favorable comments of its enthusiastic reviewers did not touch off any general popular interest in *Moby-Dick:* In the year that *Uncle Tom's Cabin* sold hundreds of thousands and *The Scarlet Letter* five thousand copies, two thousand copies of this book were adequate for the American market. And with the passage of time, the early negative judgment of *Moby-Dick* chased out the positive one. The publication of Melville's far more deeply unpopular *Pierre; or, The Ambiguities,* one year after *Moby-Dick,* clinched his reputation as a novelist who had willfully wandered from his genuine talent for exotic travel narrative into a morass of literary and philosophical experimentalism. With the consolidation of this reading of his career, Melville's more adventurous writings — *Mardi, Pierre,* and *Moby-Dick* — were consigned to the category of monstrosities or mistakes. And when this happened, they simply ceased to be read. *Uncle Tom's Cabin* kept its mass audience all through the nineteenth century as a staple of popular culture; *The Scarlet Letter,* early identified as an American classic, had a smaller but still steady readership throughout this time. But reports of nineteenth-century readings of *Moby-Dick* after 1851 are so rare as to be collector's items. It had a handful of admirers in England and Scotland in the later nineteenth century, but in America it virtually disappeared from view. Undiscussed and unread, *Moby-Dick* became, for sixty years after it was published, something like a nonexistent book.

Buried in this way, *Moby-Dick* had to await the literary changes of the early twentieth century to bring it recognition. The urge of critics of this time to search the American literary past for great works not admitted to our official culture led serious readers to look again at a forgotten book like *Moby-Dick*. And the modernist revolution created, among its other products, a new set of terms in which the book so retrieved could be appreciated. When qualities like discontinuous or fragmented form, symbolic structure, stylistic thickness, and antitraditional experiment were established as literary values, *Moby-Dick*'s peculiarities could be reinterpreted as marks of greatness, not incorrigibility. As this new code of literary values came to prevail, *Moby-Dick*'s prestige grew accordingly. Long exiled from praise, the book was hailed by the revisionist critic John Macy in 1913 as Melville's "madly eloquent romance of the sea." Four years later it received a more official form of rehabilitation when Carl Van Doren, writing in the *Cambridge History of American Literature*, called it a work of "immense originality" belonging with "the greatest sea romances in the whole history of the world."[14] In the decade that followed Melville became, for the first time, the subject of serious and sustained critical work. And as he drew new critical attention, he simultaneously returned to life for readers more generally. Justice Oliver Wendell Holmes's 1921 comment – "It's wonderful that a book published in 1851 doesn't seem thin, now. Hawthorne did when I last read *The Scarlet Letter*. Not so *Moby Dick*"[15] – can be taken as representative of the renewed power of *Moby-Dick* for its newly created modern audience after 1920. Hart Crane and William Faulkner, two other new readers of *Moby-Dick* at this time, remind us that when Melville regained this power he also became an inspiration to other writers.

The cumulative consequence of these modern developments is that *Moby-Dick* has become, in modernity, the nineteenth-century classic it never was in the nineteenth century. And even among such classics, *Moby-Dick* has had a peculiarly comprehensive form of cultural life. *Moby-Dick* has become, as much as any of our classics, a standard school text. (Nothing would have surprised Melville more than the fact that it has turned out to be *Moby-Dick*, not *Typee*, that goes down to children – and not with their gingerbread, but with the more solemn meal of compulsory reading.) But it is also true of *Moby-Dick*, as it is of few other classics, that it has been absorbed into American folklore – so much so that peo-

18

ple who have never seen a copy of *Moby-Dick* know who Captain Ahab is and use the chase of the great white whale as a metaphor for the obsessive pursuit of irrational goals. Similarly, *Moby-Dick* has become a central object of academic scholarship and criticism in the last forty years − so much so that Harry Levin could joke that Melville scholarship had replaced whaling as one of the local industries of New England. But it is also the case that *Moby-Dick*, peculiarly among America's acknowledged classics, has continued to inspire the more idiosyncratic interpretations of readers whose literary imaginations (like Melville's own) are ardent, inventive, and institutionally untrained. We owe the Melville we now know to a host of academic scholars too numerous to name here; but we owe him equally to writers like D. H. Lawrence, who gave a great early account of Melville in *Studies in Classic American Literature* (1923); to the poet Charles Olson, whose *Call Me Ishmael* (1947) is an authentic classic of Melville criticism; and to the West Indian politician, historian, and sportswriter C. L. R. James, whose study *Mariners and Renegades* (1952) cleared a path toward the sort of social reading of Melville to which criticism now shows signs of returning.

In view of the voluminous work that has been done on Melville since his revival earlier in this century, it might seem that a new volume of essays is the last thing *Moby-Dick* needs today. But this is not as true as it seems. For one thing, *Moby-Dick*, like any other object of our attention, is always in danger of hardening into a partial and official version of itself unless the act of reassessment is frequently and vigorously renewed. And in the case of *Moby-Dick* there are reasons why this renewal of inquiry is especially needed now. Precisely because *Moby-Dick* has received so much earlier attention, criticism in the last ten or fifteen years has shown signs of steering clear of the novel, as if fearing that the store of new insights had been exhausted. But this strategy has created the paradoxical result that *Moby-Dick*, although still treated as a central text, has failed either to benefit from the innovations in critical study in the last decades or to be reconnected, through renewed interpretation, with the concerns that are central to us now. The new essays collected here each concentrate on some phase of Melville's effort of imagination in *Moby-Dick:* James McIntosh's, on the nature and meaning of *Moby-Dick*'s heterogeneity; Lawrence Buell's and (from a quite different perspective) T. Walter Herbert's, on *Moby-Dick* as an act of religious imagination; Carolyn Porter's, on Melville's ways of invoking and reworking the languages or discourses of his culture; Bryan Wolf's, on Melville's engagement with the ego inflations of the romantic sublime. But what these essays have in common, and what might be said to justify them, is that each of them strives to determine what is central to *Moby-Dick* and to identify what makes Melville's work impressive now.

So conceived, these essays can stand as a modern contribution to the work that Melville's first readers began and that his early twentieth-century rediscoverers then renewed: the work of subjecting *Moby-Dick* to the kind of vigorous and many-minded interrogation that Melville's book wants and needs. If there is a further thing to be said about them, it is that as they are not the first, so they do not wish to be taken as the last word on this subject. Like Melville's Ishmael they make their various statements about *Moby-Dick* as authoritatively as they can, but in full knowledge that their object is larger than any one statement that can be made about it. Like Ishmael too, they put forth their points of view as persuasively as they know how, but as much with the hope of inciting the reader to form his own point of view as of making him accept their own ideas intact. They are essays in the root sense of tries or attempts, as in the Melvillean locution, "I try all things; I achieve what I can" (Chap. 79). And their real aim is to reanimate the trying of *Moby-Dick:* to incite readers to that active, ongoing effort to grasp a rich but elusive object that was Melville's work in *Moby-Dick* itself.

NOTES

1. Charles Olson makes the point that, in economic terms, the whaling industry was less the sequel to mercantile ventures like the China trade than the forerunner of the modern petroleum industry. Olson's discussion of the economics of whaling is a valuable treatment of an overlooked topic; see *Call Me Ishmael* (San Francisco: City Lights, 1947), pp. 16–25.

2. Michael Paul Rogin, *Subversive Genealogy: The Politics and Art of Herman Melville* (New York: Alfred A. Knopf, 1983); Ann Douglas, *The Feminization of American Culture* (New York: Alfred A. Knopf, 1977), especially chap. 9.

3. Merrell R. Davis and William H. Gilman, eds., *The Letters of Herman Melville* (New Haven, Conn.: Yale University Press, 1960), p. 39.

4. *Mardi, and a Voyage Thither* (New York: Library of America, 1982), p. 1256.

5. Davis and Gilman, eds., *Letters of Herman Melville*, p. 77.

6. Melville, "Hawthorne and His Mosses," p. 1169. I use the text of this essay as it appears in the third Library of America volume of Melville's complete prose (New York, 1984).

7. Jay Leyda, ed., *The Melville Log: A Documentary Life of Herman Melville*, rev. ed., vol. 2 (New York: Gordian Press, 1969), p. 529.

8. Ibid., p. 926.

9. "Hawthorne and His Mosses," pp. 1159, 1160.

10. Davis and Gilman, eds., *Letters of Herman Melville*, p. 143; Leyda, ed., *Melville Log*, 1:412.

11. Davis and Gilman, eds., *Letters of Herman Melville*, p. 130.

12. Early reviews of *Moby-Dick* are collected in several volumes: in Hershel Parker, ed., *The Recognition of Herman Melville* (Ann Arbor: University of Michigan Press, 1967); Hershel Parker and Harrison Hayford, eds., *Moby-Dick as Doubloon: Essays and Extracts (1851–1970)* (New York: W. W. Norton, 1970); and Watson G. Branch, ed., *Melville: The Critical Heritage* (London: Routledge and Kegan Paul, 1974). These quotations come from the reviews in the Washington *National Intelligencer* and the English periodical *John Bull*, reprinted in *Melville: The Critical Heritage*, pp. 283 and 256.

13. See *Melville: The Critical Heritage*, pp. 254, 253, 333, and 267.

14. John Macy, *The Spirit of American Literature* (New York: Doubleday, Page, 1913), p. 16. Van Doren's remarks are reprinted in *The Recognition of Herman Melville*, pp. 153–154.

15. Cited in Jay B. Hubbell, *Who Are the Major American Writers?* (Durham, N.C.: Duke University Press, 1972), p. 62. On the modern revival of Melville, see *The Recognition of Herman Melville*, pp. vii–xii and 153–206, and Hubbell, pp. 57–63.

2

The Mariner's Multiple Quest

JAMES MCINTOSH

AS much as any key work of fiction in English in the mid-nineteenth century, Melville's *Moby-Dick* is open to religious and psychological uncertainty. Ishmael claims early that he was "born and bred in the bosom of the infallible Presbyterian Church" (Chap. 10), and Melville himself was likewise nurtured in orthodox Calvinism by his Dutch Reformed mother and minister; yet by the time he wrote *Moby-Dick*, he had not only lived among cannibals and whalemen but had "swam through libraries" (Chap. 32). The peculiarities of his mariner's experience and his self-education left him untethered, open to "divine intuitions" from all quarters (Chap. 85). He embraced his uncertainties enthusiastically, not unhappily, as he might five years later when, as Hawthorne noted, "He can neither believe, nor be comfortable in his unbelief."[1]

In the spring of 1851, perhaps at the height of Melville's and Hawthorne's friendship for each other, Sophia Hawthorne wrote of her intriguing neighbor, "Melville's fresh, sincere, glowing mind . . . is in a state of 'fluid consciousness,' & to Mr. Hawthorne speaks his innermost about GOD, the Devil, & Life if so be he can get at the Truth for he is a boy in opinion — having settled nothing yet."[2] Mrs. Hawthorne is wary of Melville, but also responsive to what is crucially alive in him. When she lights on the words "fluid consciousness," she describes a characteristic of his mind that pervades not only his fiction but all his writings of the period. The phrase, I surmise, is adapted from Emerson, who wrote, "Nature is not fixed but fluid" as well as "there are no fixtures to man, if we appeal to consciousness";[3] and it is suggestive that she would draw on Emerson to describe Melville. Emerson too takes uncertainty amid the breakdown of traditional belief as the condition for

23

his endeavor, and glories in the fluidity of mind available to self-emancipated young Americans. Melville in the early 1850s is not only a privileged isolato who has cut the umbilical cord to his culture and questioned its received assumptions, but also an exemplary American writer in his pleasure in change and fluidity. His mind is always in transit. He savors "temporary feeling" as he contemplates a lovely landscape, but is wary of the "universal application" of such a mood, lest it lead to self-deception. Similarly, his social affections are marked by the truth of the moment. He writes Hawthorne, "In me divine magnanimities are spontaneous and instantaneous − catch them while you can."[4] And on all ideological questions he is in search of a viewpoint − he has "settled nothing yet." It should not surprise us, then, that *Moby-Dick* itself is a book in transit, in search of its own meaning, not subject to neat resolution.

This fluidity or multiplicity of mind is expressed in many ways in *Moby-Dick*. To begin with, Melville is a multiply minded scourer of libraries. He is willing to accommodate a multitude of sources in the fabric of the book, alternatively using and testing them in a process of continuous exploration and reconstitution. Very quickly, the book advertises its openness to a host of perspectives in the Extracts, an anthology of passages on the whale culled from old books and new. Indeed, *Moby-Dick* is, among other things, an encyclopedia of extracts. In his review, Evert Duyckinck called it, half-disparagingly, "an intellectual chowder."[5] Duyckinck had been Melville's friend, but Melville's freedom of mind alarmed him; yet he is getting at an essential quality of the book. One of Melville's purposes is to compose a reflective compendium of the texts available to him from European and American culture at this point in his intellectual development. He takes it on himself not only to gather together as much of his reading as possible, but also to juxtapose texts and let them comment on each other, to rewrite key texts such as "The Rime of the Ancient Mariner" and subvert others, such as the Book of Jonah, for his own purposes. As a result, *Moby-Dick*, like Shelley's *Prometheus Unbound* or Goethe's *Faust*, is a critical synthesis of its culture's literature. Such "chowders" are something new in literary history (no wonder they baffled early readers) but appropriate and timely creations for writers who wished to use their multifarious reading as a means of intellectual and religious liberation.

Melville's many-sidedness and his lability of mind are apparent not only in his extracts and allusions but also in the texture of his meditations and dramatic scenes. His spontaneous energy of mind leads to a particular kind of dramatic instability in the novel. In individual scenes crucial to the action, Melville sets up moods only to disrupt them. The reader is not to bask in any given mood long enough to get attached to it or become oblivious to the need for change. When the grand armada of whales collects unexpectedly around an enchanted center of calm, we savor only briefly the privileges of insight at that center. Ishmael no sooner reports how "deep inland" he bathes "in eternal mildness of joy" (Chap. 87) than he is forced to abandon this serenity. A stricken whale recalls him from his abstraction by flailing a harpoon bloodily among his fellows, testing the vigilance of boat crews and readers alike. Rapturous assurances of the peace to be found in nature are offered temporarily, only to be disrupted, here and elsewhere in *Moby-Dick*. In "A Squeeze of the Hand" Ishmael gets carried away in a natural rapture when he squeezes the "sperm" of a dead whale. "For the time" he lives "as in a musky meadow" (Chap. 94) and forgets about his oath of vengeance. His feelings of affection and freedom from malice are genuine, for the moment at least; they point to a change of heart that may save him eventually; yet they are not only temporary but suspect in that they are accompanied by "a strange sort of insanity," which he acts out comically by fondling the hands of his shipmates. Melville does not allow the reader to get hamstrung in a single thematic pattern. If his thrust here seems at first hopeful but then more questionable, elsewhere he proceeds oppositely, from apparent pessimism to a measured optimism. In "The Try-Works" Ishmael reports how "for the time" he felt deadened by apprehensions of woe until he shook free of them. Mesmerized by "the face of the fire" (Chap. 96), he fell asleep at the tiller and only saved himself and the ship by a timely self-recovery. Again he finds sanity in change, only temporary truth in singlemindedness.

Melville's fluidity of mind is also expressed in his penchant for attaching multiple, incrementally accretive significance to key im-

25

ages in the action. When, for instance, Ishmael first reports on the white scar that marks Ahab's face and neck, he not only makes the reader see it vividly but also sets up a train of unresolved speculation in connection with it. The scar is interpreted and/or imagined in several ways. To the Manxman, it is the exposed part of a birthmark that covers Ahab "from crown to sole"; to an old Gay-Head Indian, it is the result of "an elemental strife at sea" (Chap. 28). The narrator, rather than deciding on one of these readings, complicates the issue by associating the scar with another natural phenomenon – it resembles the "perpendicular seam" of a great tree branded by lightning.

Melville may well have learned from Hawthorne the technique of multiple explanations for the physical manifestations of the secret workings of the human heart. Yet Melville's use of alternative explanations is subtly different from Hawthorne's and reveals a fluid consciousness at work rather than the precisely selecting mind of an anatomist and historian of the psyche. The passage on the scar is open-ended. Speculation about it remains fluid when one reads the paragraph. We suspend disbelief in the superstitious supposals of these old sailors and entertain their explanations as possibilities for the fiction ahead of us. The implied author does not pose as an ironist between the lines, teasing the reader into his own thought, as Hawthorne might, but presents himself through his narrator as a skeptical but sympathetic reporter of all possibilities.

In similar fashion, Melville has us read other images syntagmatically and metonymically, with a fluid consciousness of our own. The spirit spout first appears to be "a silvery jet"; seems then "some plumed and glittering god uprising from the sea"; seems an evil spirit summoned as well as descried by Fedallah; seems Moby-Dick himself; makes the crew instinctively eager to lower at night against their custom – they feel "no terror, rather pleasure"; yet seems, as the voyage narrative rapidly unfolds in the chapter, to lead the *Pequod* across vast seas to confront "sights more dismal than before" – inscrutable ravens, cold seas and storms, "demoniac waves" (Chap. 51). Or the whale's skeleton in "A Bower in the Arsacides" is portrayed successively as a religious ikon foisted on innocent islanders by the priests of Tranque; as a splendid natural

object set amid a magnificent carpet of vegetation in the Arsacidean wood; as a "a gigantic idler" — the object now personified
and dramatized; as himself the begetter or "cunning weaver" of
that gorgeous carpet; and as just a skeleton ("naught was there
but bones" [Chap. 102]). Concerning these several expansions on
an image — scar, spout, skeleton — we may well hope, with Ishmael, that "Surely all this is not without meaning" (Chap. 1). But
though we properly seek ways of explaining the presentation of
each of these, the text in every case militates against univocal
interpretation. What's the reason Ishmael goes to sea? Already in
"Loomings" he gives many reasons in a casual-seeming order.

By refusing to pin down the meanings of his images definitively,
Melville runs the danger of having them mean nothing at all. This
possibility is raised almost systematically in "The Doubloon." At
the start of that chapter, Ishmael restates his own insistent hope for
meaning: "And some certain significance lurks in all things, else
all things are little worth, and the round world itself but an empty
cipher, except to sell by the cartload, as they do hills about Boston,
to fill up some morass in the Milky Way" (Chap. 99). But by the
chapter's end, the round doubloon seems but a cipher indeed. At a
crucial point Stubb observes the Manxman reading the doubloon
as a sign and portent of impending doom. Stubb's comment here is
pertinent to the whole of *Moby-Dick:* "There's another rendering
now; but still one text. All sorts of men in one kind of world, you
see." We will shortly observe how different characters "render"
differently not just single images but the voyage of the *Pequod* as a
whole, and how this complexity of perspective is crucial to the
book's structure. Yet the book also poses the question of whether
such a jumbling of views has any value. One inference that might
be drawn from Stubb's remark is that all renderings of any given
text are equally specious. In "The Doubloon" itself, complexity is
reduced to a polysemous gibberish. As Pip madly concludes when
he sums up the scene, "I look, you look, he looks; we look, ye
look, they look." Different perspectives cancel each other out and
build to no meaning.

Yet, though the nihilistic relativism Pip voices is one philosophical possibility that *Moby-Dick* indeed posits, the book does not rest
in nihilism any more than in the other attitudes it temporarily

27

takes. "The Doubloon" offers not a conclusive summing up of the book's epistemology but one way among several of dealing with the multiplicity and mutability of human perceptions. Like "Loomings" or "The Sermon" or "The Grand Armada" or "The Try-Works," it is another experiment in imagining the same voyage. None of these experiments is final in itself, and none entirely displaces or discredits the others. Melville's imagination is accumulative as well as deconstructive. As he evokes the scar or the spirit spout, he glories in accumulated connotation. The doubloon is hardly typical in that it is emptied of connotation in the course of its inspection and analysis.

Melville's openness to possibility threatens at times to bring his book to the edge of nihilism, as if the doubloon, in its diverse meanings, meant nothing and the variegated world were only a meretricious illusion hiding a blankness at the core. Yet "The Doubloon" and "The Whiteness of the Whale," though they are certainly meant to scare us, are from a global perspective temporary resting places in the total reading *Moby-Dick*. At other points the reader, prompted by a mood of the narrator or a turn in the story, is properly more sanguine. If Ishmael succombs to a hypo in "The Whiteness of the Whale," he is speculatively optimistic in "The Fountain," for the moment at peace with his labile condition. As he puts it jocosely and seriously, "through all the thick mists of the dim doubts in my mind, divine intuitions now and then shoot, enkindling my fog with a heavenly ray. And for this I thank God; for all have doubts; many deny; but doubts or denials, few along with them, have intuitions. Doubts of all things earthly, and intuitions of some things heavenly; this combination makes neither believer nor infidel, but makes a man who regards them both with equal eye" (Chap. 85).

The willingness to be open both to doubts and "now and then" to restorative intuitions helps generate the enormous inventiveness of language and thought in *Moby-Dick,* its wealth of connotation and speculation. Yet even if we reject Pip's relativism as a form of overly lucid madness or Ishmael's argument for whiteness as a rationalization on the part of a temporarily craven soul, we are still left with the problem of finding a model for interpreting fluid consciousness. How can Melville "settle nothing yet" and still give direction to his plot, balance to his conflicting and multiple ways of thinking, and wholeness to his thematic design? How can the reader find form in Melville's multiplicity? To answer such questions will be my task in the rest of this essay.

In its narrative form, *Moby-Dick* fits the traditional literary form of a quest romance. It is a voyage or quest to slay a monster – the White Whale; to explore a distant place or underworld in search of a treasure or secret; and to use that secret to redeem common existence – in the book's terms to restore "antique Adam" (Chap. 7) and his many descendants to their rights in a heartless universe. In the period of literary romanticism, during which *Moby-Dick* appears as a late efflorescence, traditional romance often takes on the character of an "internalized quest," in Harold Bloom's phrase.[6] Romantic protagonists such as Shelley's Prometheus or Blake's Los or Goethe's Faust or Poe's Arthur Gordon Pym are engaged in internal searches for spiritual health or experience or knowledge. Descents to an underworld, whether imagined mythologically, like Faust's journey to the realm of the Mothers, or "realistically," like Pym's sea voyage to the South Pole, are on one level patent allegories of inward exploration. Wordsworth's *Prelude* and Thoreau's *Walden* are both extended journeys back to where these thoughtful saunterers started from, to places they knew as children where they can recover their imaginative wholeness. Carlyle's Diogenes Teufelsdrökh is not only a Professor of Things in General but also a wanderer who discovers the soul. Sometimes a romantic quest evolves into a search for ambiguous or destructive knowledge, as in Coleridge's "Rime of the Ancient Mariner," Byron's *Cain*, and *Moby-Dick* itself. At least three internalized quests – "The Rime of the Ancient Mariner," *Sartor Resartus*, and *Faust* – are key sources for *Moby-Dick*. Others, like *The Narrative of Arthur Gordon Pym*, are at least significant analogues. Yet in one respect, Melville's masterpiece is a new invention in romanticism, intuitively created to express his particular kind of imagination.

As far as I know, *Moby-Dick* is virtually unique in romantic literature in that it is a multiple, not a singular, quest. With the peculiar exception of Blake's epics, the other quest romances I have referred to, whether autobiographical or fictional, affirming or ambiguous, have one central protagonist. Wordsworth and Thoreau pursue enlightenment alone in their poetic autobiographies. The ancient mariner is the only mariner who counts in Coleridge's *Rime*. In *Prometheus Unbound* and *Faust*, other figures are ancillary to the titular hero. In *Sartor Resartus* the English editor is but a gentle foil to the German professor. In *Moby-Dick*, by contrast, many characters are on separate though interrelated voyages, pursuing a host of internal secrets. The White Whale is one thing to Ahab and something else "at times" to Ishmael (Chap. 42) – fluid-minded Ishmael keeps his options open. These are the two fictive persons on whom Melville lavishes most attention. But in key, poetically rich passages, Melville projects other mini-quests: Bulkington on a voyage past the rocks of the lee shore, or Pip descending to the depths of the primal world, or Queequeg meeting the infinite horizon in his totemic canoe. Early in the book, Father Mapple preaches a Christian version of the voyage against which the *Pequod*'s vindictive mission is set in ironic contrast. Even on the ship, Mapple's Christian structuring of the voyage receives momentary lyrical expression in Captain Bildad's hymn, "Sweet fields beyond the swelling flood." Finally (though not exhaustively), the crew of the *Pequod* as an aggregate has its own unconscious purpose as it pursues not just Moby-Dick but all whales. Indeed, in my own most recent reading, the crew has seemed a third chief protagonist alongside Ishmael and Ahab, almost as important as they in creating the mixed effect of the whole voyage.

When I speak of "the mariner's multiple quest," however, I mean not only to pay respects to "Coleridge's wild Rhyme" (Chap. 42) but also to suggest that ultimately one imagination travels on all these voyages. *Moby-Dick* has a kind of associative unity in that its various characters keep investigating the same phenomena and noumena – one whale, one White Whale, one doubloon, one ungraspable phantom, and one sea, however many the renderings of these texts. As Melville writes and we read, characters tend to get linked to each other because they are faced repeatedly with similar questions or because a character embodies a problem or need for another character. There is a hidden fraternity among these shipmates: Ahab projects himself on Fedallah, Pip, and Starbuck; Ishmael imagines himself as Queequeg, Pip, and Bulkington, as well as the rest of the crew, and acknowledges his kinship to Ahab; Queequeg is at times his own man, whereas at other times he melds with his fellow harpooners Tashtego and Daggoo. We should be careful to keep these characters separate as well as fusing them. Each lives as a minute particular in Melville's imagination. Nevertheless, formally this is a quest romance, not (however rich its social implications) a novel of society that depends for its plot on the depiction of class differences between characters. One imagination is at work on a heterogeneous collection of needs in an attempt to comprehend and encircle the aggregate need of those who travel on the *Pequod*. Moreover, Melville shares the Emersonian romantic assumption that each person and each fictional character not only has a soul of his own but also acts as a representative of "the soul" that all of us share. The book is a many-headed representation of the soul engaged in a single, if multifaceted, adventure. Hence one "mariner" on a group of interrelated voyages, hence a "multiple quest."

Before we examine these different voyages, we should try to understand something of their interrelation. To restate the last paragraph, men put to sea in *Moby-Dick* for a common set of reasons varied to suit the dispositions and conscious or unconscious designs of particular voyagers. An array of these reasons is offered in "Loomings," before any voyaging begins. Though Ishmael speaks for himself there, he hints at questions posed in fragmentary form in the context of other voyages as well. First, how does one deal with the prospect of death? On shore Ishmael pauses before coffin warehouses and brings up the rear of funerals. At sea a mariner apparently feels the better for having to imagine death at close hand. Second, how does one confront one's "hypos," one's potential for unconscious derangement and ultimately for madness? This too we hide from ourselves on shore and face more immediately at sea. Madness seems an immediate presence on the *Pequod*; Ahab embodies that prospect and danger for the crew. Madness is in fact a danger for all who acknowledge the unknown deep within themselves. As Ishmael puts it whimsically when he observes Queequeg's Ramadan, "we are all somehow dreadfully cracked about the head, and sadly need mending" (Chap. 17). Third, how does one deal with the strangeness of nature — with the material sea itself, with the landscape and its beauty and terror, with animals, and with one's own body, a palpable natural enigma in the unknown circumstances of voyaging? Natural strangeness, in one respect epitomized by the whale, may seem to oppose the mariner, or he may like it. Ishmael is "quick to perceive a horror, and could still be social with it." "Wild and distant seas" and "barbarous coasts" appeal to him (Chap. 1). That wildness, of course, speaks to an answering wildness in human nature; so the quest is on one level an exploration of the primitive power in man and the sea. More to be feared than nature's wildness and strangeness, however, is its possible meaninglessness. A fourth reason for going to sea — and this too is suggested in "Loomings" — is to try to give it meaning. Fifth, at least Ishmael and the crew go to sea to work and get paid for it. Their voyage brings practical as well as mysterious knowledge — one learns of the whale through work — and brings incidental fleshly pleasures like a whale steak, a tot of rum, or a social smoke, else the crew and the reader too would scorn its unreality. But this practical reason for the voyage rubs shoulders with less tangible reasons and leads to the question, how does one use work and pleasure and the things one works with or enjoys in the search for truth? Finally, at the other end of the tangible–intangible spectrum, the mariner on this voyage openly pursues "the tormenting mild image" of himself — as Narcissus did and, like Bulkington, was drowned for it. This "ungraspable phantom of life" (Chap. 1) may be only in one's head, but in *Moby-Dick* a sea voyage leads there as well as to the Line south of Japan.

The multiple quest in *Moby-Dick,* then, not only is embodied in various versions but also has many purposes. One goes to sea for many reasons. These reasons come into play side by side in Melville's prose because his imagination of the voyage is "fluid" — nowhere more freely and zestfully so than in "Loomings." Melville's mariner is impelled to seek knowledge on a variety of fronts, to know what death might mean and what awaits us on the frontiers of consciousness; to know the barbarous and strange in man and beyond him; and to know ordinary nature and ordinary work. By association, Melville puts forth an implicit structure of knowledge, spreading that structure in loosely connected fragmentary ideas across several pages. Such a structure operates subliminally throughout the book once it is set up in the first chapter. The chapter itself creates an impression of wholeness despite its heterogeneity. In it a mentally adventurous youth reflects on all that he needs to make him a whole man — bread as well as ungraspable phantoms.

To illustrate the multiple quest, I begin with Queequeg's imagined voyage in "Queequeg in His Coffin." In a sense, the choice is arbitrary — not the first narrative of a voyage (that would be Father Mapple's story of Jonah), not necessarily a key component of the main narrative, almost a random example, though I trust in its own way a paradigmatic one. It is typical of all shorter versions of the quest — indeed, of all of Melville's interpolated stories of whaling ships and whalemen — in that it is a voyage within a voyage, an independent narrative that appears without obvious preparation in the midst of a fluid whole. From the *Pequod*'s fixed station on the sea you can start out for anywhere, illustrate in yet another way what it means to go a-whaling.

The narrative returns to Queequeg after neglecting him for many pages. The occasion for bringing him in is, as usual, the work of a whaler; but from an account of workaday business the narrative slides easily into a symbolic evocation of Queequeg's being and his imaginative needs. He catches a fever while hoisting casks and searching for leaks deep in the ship's interior. As he works to save the ship, he appears not only as a valiant, reliable harpooner but also as a comic spectacle: "Stripped to his woollen drawers, the tattooed savage was crawling about amid that dampness and slime, like a green spotted lizard at the bottom of a well" (Chap. 110). This comic emphasis serves to set the account of Queequeg's conception of a totemic canoe that follows apart from other accounts of imaginative conception and longing in the book. Queequeg is not a New Englander like Ishmael or Ahab or Starbuck or Father Mapple, but a "poor pagan." He looks like a green lizard because he has tattoos on his legs like "dark green frogs . . . running up the trunks of young palms" (Chap. 3). His voyage, then, is a pagan version of the general voyage. He acts "cracked about the head" in the style of a South Sea Islander, with an eccentricity of behavior that seems to displace all hypos. When he falls ill, it will likewise be in his own strange manner – suddenly, unpredictably, impressively. He wastes away

> till there seemed but little left of him but his frame and tattooing. But as all else in him thinned, and his cheekbones grew sharper, his eyes, nevertheless, seemed growing fuller and fuller; they became of a strange softness of lustre; and mildly but deeply looked out at you there from his sickness, a wondrous testimony to that immortal health in him which could not die, or be weakened. And like circles on the water, which, as they grow fainter, expand; so his eyes seemed rounding and rounding like the rings of Eternity. (Chap. 110)

"The drawing near of Death" seems to bring a preternatural serenity to his pagan mind. By courtesy of Ishmael's metaphors, we sense that Queequeg is already on his distinctive voyage. In Queequeg's eyes, Ishmael contemplates an opening out of "the rings of Eternity," a movement of circles expanding ever more faintly into a distance toward the horizon between life and death. Such imagery of circular expansion toward endlessness joins other imagery of movement conveying Queequeg's state of mind. Ishmael sees "mysterious shades" of "holier thoughts" "creeping over the face of poor Queequeg, as he quietly lay in his swaying hammock, and the rolling sea seemed gently rocking him to his final rest, and the ocean's invisible flood-tide lifted him higher and higher toward his destined heaven." The actual direction of all these motions – "rounding . . . swaying . . . rolling . . . rocking" and lifting "towards his destined heaven" is properly obscure and overdetermined, since it represents "thoughts," not physical activity. But these words of motion, imitative of a ship's movement at sea perhaps, prepare us for the specific death voyage Queequeg plans for himself.

He chooses, we recall, to be placed in a coffin-canoe with biscuits and water for sustenance on his journey, and "woody earth" at his feet and sail cloth under his head as signs of his origin and his calling. He prepares for death with a quintessentially pagan rite. Not only like the Polynesian he is, but like an American Indian or an Egyptian, he would take tokens of life into the shades beyond. For Melville, "pagan" implies ease in one's intercourse with the natural world, including one's passage into nature at death. Queequeg constructs "nature" in his imagination so as to be at home in it. He would avoid sharks, but otherwise this journey of dying and death harbors no terrors for him. He follows "the custom of his own race" in planning a sea voyage in his improvised canoe to "the starry archipelagoes; for not only do they believe that the stars are isles, but that far beyond all visible horizons, their own mild, uncontinented seas, interflow with the blue heavens; and so form the white breakers of the milky way" (Chap. 110).

All such imagery indicates a modulation into an extraordinary mildness in the midst of the *Pequod*'s vindictive voyaging. "The white breakers of the milky way" bring to Queequeg thoughts of congenial and familiar waters, not, as to Ishmael earlier, thoughts of white annihilation (Chap. 42). Queequeg's imagination of death in his voyage is in one sense too strange to imitate. Only he has a "complete" and unreadable "theory of the heavens and the earth" (Chap. 110) inscribed on the surface of his body, suggesting not so much that he is illiterate as that he possesses a primal knowledge – he is in touch with a meaning for his round world even though he cannot read the hieroglyphic tattoos that incorporate that meaning. Yet, in another sense, he represents one pole of possible understanding for the mariner and the reader in *Moby-Dick*. He is not only a pagan but also a whaleman who has shipped aboard the *Pequod*. His coffin-canoe, like a whale boat, lacks a keel, and may involve "but uncertain steering, and much lee-way adown the dim ages." By giving such a turn to Queequeg's ideas, Melville brings him closer to the rest of the crew and to the reader. For all his serenity, he too sails into uncertainty.

Moreover, as Queequeg enacts his version of the voyage, he fulfills in his own way the different functions of the mariner's quest. He deflects sickness and madness, contrives a strategy for dealing with death, makes material objects and articles pertaining to the work of a whaler into vehicles of meaning, and adopts a particular stance toward the strangeness of nature. Ishmael's rationale for going to sea in "Loomings" is thus linked to Queequeg's unconscious purpose in imagining his voyage. This linkage is of a piece with Melville's effort in the whole book to see Queequeg as one possible manifestation of "soul." "You cannot hide the soul" says Ishmael when he learns to see human nature in Queequeg's face (Chap. 10). Ishmael not only becomes Queequeg's bosom friend, but later in the book avers that he means to cover his own body with a tattooed poem and claims that he is himself a savage, "owning no allegiance but to the King of the Cannibals" (Chaps. 102, 57). These boasts are not only whimsical posturings for the reader but also gestures of fraternity for Queequeg. On the multiple quest, Queequeg represents for the soul a possibility of pagan health, of unalienated savage ease in nature. His fantasy voyage directs him toward a heaven indivisible from his familiar ocean world.

It is suggestive for my purposes that mad Pip also figures prominently in "Queequeg in His Coffin." Pip's appearance in the chapter invites the reader to compare him with Queequeg. In Pip's own words, Queequeg is a hero who "dies game," whereas "base little Pip, he died a coward" (Chap. 110). But since as readers we sympathize disinterestedly with both characters, we compare them not as Pip does, as if one were a success and the other a failure, but rather as examples of how different shipmates render Melville's sea differently. The chapter reminds us not only that Pip is mad, whereas Queequeg is eccentrically sane, but also that both of these dark-complexioned outsiders contribute their versions to our total imagination of the voyage. In his babble of a monologue, Pip divines that Queequeg is bound for some serene islands of the blessed: "But if the currents carry ye to those sweet Antilles where the beaches are only beat with water-lilies, will ye do one little errand for me? Seek out one Pip, who's now been missing long." The rime of "Antilles" and "lilies" almost seems to undercut the chapter's lyricism, as if Melville through Pip were momentarily mocking the paradise Ishmael has evoked for Queequeg. Be that as it may, Pip's request is clue enough for us to seek him out at that point in the book when he "died," when he was cast away at sea and saw in his mind an undersea vision of God.

When Pip leaps from Stubb's boat, he finds himself in a very different sea from the one Queequeg envisions on his sick bed. The image of traveling into the unknown Ishmael sees in Queequeg's eyes is of circles expanding toward an eternal horizon. Pip finds himself, by contrast, a lonely self staring out at endless space. "The intense concentration of self in the middle of such a heartless immensity, my God! who can tell it?'' (Chap. 93). Queequeg constructs nature as a subjective retreat, a dwelling place for his imagination in which stars are isles and one travels into death as into something familiar. In Pip's case, the sea is not just an analogue for his terrified state of mind – though it is that – but also a landscape oppressively actual. It seems at that moment to him and Ishmael ironically beautiful but indifferent, ''calm and cool, and flatly stretching away, all round, to the horizon, like gold-beater's skin hammered out to the extremest.'' Nature has turned serene but alien in this version of the voyage. The horizon becomes for Pip an image not of peace but of abandonment. ''Pip's ringed horizon began to expand around him miserably.'' The image and phrasing recall a moment in ''Midnight, Forecastle,'' when the Old Manx sailor saw the fight between black Daggoo and a Spanish sailor in an improvised 'ring'' as an emblem of man's bloodthirstiness and of God's indifference to his own cruel creation. ''There! the ringed horizon. In that ring Cain struck Abel. Sweet work, right work! No? Why then, God, mad'st thou the ring?'' (Chap. 40).

We can compare Pip and Queequeg in terms of our paradigm from ''Loomings.'' Queequeg, wild himself, is at ease in wild nature; Pip is overwhelmed in a ''heartless'' landscape. Queequeg's gods protect him; Pip is God's (or the gods') victim. Queequeg's bizarre behavior – testing his own coffin for comfort, recovering in a day from what seemed a mortal illness, then using the coffin-canoe as a sea chest – appears a healthy way of acting out the hypos; Pip goes mad without any such recourse. Queequeg's vision is tribal and social; Pip's recognition of his loneliness comes to him because he has been abandoned, and ultimately it stems from the social fact that he is an American black without tribe or power, a victim of man's inhumanity as well as God's indifference.

Yet Pip's experience has its compensation. Ishmael first speculates on Pip's inner condition: ''The sea had jeeringly kept his finite body up, but drowned the infinite of his soul.'' Then he reverses himself, in a deservedly famous passage:

> Not drowned entirely, though. Rather carried down alive to wondrous depths, where strange shapes of the unwarped primal world glided to and fro before his passive eyes; and the miser-merman,

Wisdom, revealed his hoarded heaps; and among the joyous, heartless, ever-juvenile eternities, Pip saw the multitudinous, God-om-
nipresent, coral insects, that out of the firmament of waters heaved
the colossal orbs. He saw God's foot upon the treadle of the loom,
and spoke it; and therefore his shipmates called him mad. (Chap.
93)

Melville meditates his way into his subject, complicating his understanding not only of madness but also of the principles of creation, destiny, wisdom, and beauty — hence of God. If one sees
these impersonal principles at work weaving the world, one goes
mad from the sight of divine power. Yet Pip's plight has led to his
privileged vision; his insanity is laced with "heaven's sense."

In the face of physical danger, Pip is propelled on a voyage
within; like Queequeg later, he becomes a mental traveler. Yet
whereas Queequeg would travel across the level sea to the starry
archipelagoes or even be lifted upward to heaven, Pip's soul is
"carried down alive to wondrous depths." His vision in the depths
is another instance of the soul's reaching for a possibility of knowledge in the book. Melville explores what it might mean to go
down, go within the self, and discover there an undersea realm of
secrets intolerable to mortal reason.

If we think of the directions of these voyages as metaphors for
inner compulsions, we can also compare them fruitfully with
Bulkington's earlier voyage. Bulkington is an American, not a
Polynesian, thus an embodiment of self-reliance and not of primitive unreadable tribal wisdom. Though he, like Queequeg, sails
over and across Melville's sea, his ocean perishing brings him to
no starry islands. He represents "the intrepid effort of the soul to
keep the open independence of her sea" (Chap. 23). He is compelled to seek that open independence, not God's depths or a
tribe's paradise. In the three episodes, then, the soul is lifted to the
heights, penetrates to the depths, and strives to survive while driving across "the lashed sea's landlessness" toward a placeless visionary death. The three passages offer three different precise images of what may happen to man's inner power in extreme
circumstances. Melville inserts the passages casually at separate
points into his total narrative, with the effect that the mariner's
possibilities for inner experience appear multiple. As readers, we

never know when we will be treated to another such voyage. And indeed, we are being treated subliminally to others all the time – to Ahab's, to Ishmael's, to the crew's, at least retrospectively to Father Mapple's.

Any engaged reader of *Moby-Dick* has a sense of what propels Ahab on his voyage: his rage against a heartless universe and the gods he imagines behind it; his effort to get at hidden meanings behind the impenetrable mask of visible things; his obsession with Moby Dick, who for him embodies this malignity and impenetrability; his scorn for his own body and the body's work; and his willful disregard for "nature," for natural beauty and natural human longings despite their appeal for him. A perspective such as mine that stresses Melville's multiplicity runs the risk that Ahab will not receive his due importance. Yet a sensitivity to Melville's fluid consciousness also helps one to understand features of his procedure with Ahab. First, just as *Moby-Dick* is a compendium of previous texts reworked in a chowder of Melville's own making, so Ahab himself is a composite of earlier historical, literary, and mythical figures. He is not only a shaggy Nantucket captain whose brows congeal in a storm, not only a Quaker with a vengeance or a lonely and fierce Andrew Jackson on his war horse, but also a Jonah who doesn't come back; an unrepentant Job; a self-crucified Christ who wakes with his own bloody nails in his palms; a Faust who makes a pact with a familiar oriental devil; a Macbeth who hearkens to false assurances; a Lear whose madness is tempered by the ministrations of a mad boy who loves him; a Perseus with an ivory leg; and a Prometheus who creates his own vultures to peck at his own heart. Melville's "Ahab Americanus," like Cotton Mather's John Winthrop, is the American antitype of many earlier types.[7] This typological approach to characterization is of a piece with Melville's multiply adhesive approach to all knowledge and all earlier texts. It leads to some confusion or, perhaps, acrobatic mind stretching. Jonah, Macbeth, and Perseus hardly consort easily together. Yet Melville's intention seems to be to evoke Ahab as a gritty modern representative of all sufferers, aspirers, questers after monsters, and vengeance seekers. Insanely, Ahab would bring all their complaints and desires to the bar. The effect of these many references is to have us contemplate Ahab wonderingly within a panorama of types as well as to respond to him emotionally as to a single character, and to lend him the stature of one marked by man's perennial woes as well as the condition of a wounded cripple bearing a grudge. As the voyage proceeds, Melville gives us many perspectives on Ahab, holding him up as a figure of incalculable, demoniac force, gradually humanizing him when he responds humanly to other characters, yet pointing up his folly along with his pride, so that in our wondering detachment we feel a combination of admiration, sympathy, and contempt for this strange composite quester.

Second, since *Moby-Dick* is a multiple voyage, the text asks the reader over and over to compare Ahab with his fellow voyagers. They are all foils for him, even or especially in their differences from him. Ahab's central voyage appears in relief when contrasted to Queequeg's — not only Queequeg's imagined journey into death but his joint tour of duty with Ishmael on the *Pequod* and his voyage as a primitive harpooner with Tashtego and Daggoo. (Queequeg too is presented to the reader from varying perspectives.) While Queequeg is at work on the ship, he treats the natural world as a world of fellow creatures. He has no fear of phantoms or hatred of symbolic beasts. His kinship with "the heavens and the earth" baffles and goads Ahab, who sees the unreadable hieroglyphics on Queequeg's body as an infuriating natural mystery, a "devilish tantalization of the gods" (Chap. 110), not as an ever-present reminder of ancestral wisdom. Yet for all their difference, Queequeg is one of Ahab's crew, engaged in the communal fiery hunt for Moby Dick. On that voyage his individual character is sacrificed, and he points up Ahab's power. Inversely, Ahab is strongly linked by ties of affection to Pip, yet ultimately sets himself apart from him. And the book early makes clear their difference as well as their likeness. The "brightness" (Chap. 93) of Pip's intellect is obscured in his madness, whereas in Ahab's "broad madness, not one jot of his great natural intellect had perished" (Chap. 41). On the other hand, Pip has an innocence that makes possible his redeeming epiphany in the presence of God's power. Ahab's venture into the unknown and the deep has brought him no such compensation. His agony and hatred are correspondingly more intense and awesome. Pip's bout with divinity only points up Ahab's willful ultimate loneliness.

In his vindictive approach to the sea, Ahab is successively set apart from all other figures on the *Pequod*, though all follow his lead, perhaps out of a secret vindictiveness of their own. Likewise, his voyage differs from those of all the captains he meets at all the gams the *Pequod* enters into while at sea. Above all, perhaps, Ahab's voyage is to be defined in terms of its difference from and likeness to the voyage of Father Mapple's Calvinized Jonah, which Mapple narrates in his sermon to his captive audience of fellow whalemen early in the book.

We are apt to interpret Father Mapple's sermon simply as the expression of a Christian message that Ahab scorns and Ishmael and Queequeg willfully ignore. After all, Queequeg shows his indifference to the sermon by leaving the chapel some time before the benediction, and though Ishmael stays to hear Mapple out, upon his return to the Spouter Inn he enters into a blasphemous pact of bosom friendship with Queequeg that mocks Mapple's message. Ishmael and Queequeg smoke together and embrace; Queequeg gives Ishmael a present of an embalmed head; and they divvy up between them Queequeg's thirty pieces of silver – the wages of Judas turned to benevolent pagan ends. We might infer, then, that their voyage together on the *Pequod* represents a betrayal of Christianity, or (if one sides with them) Ishmael's means of liberation from Presbyterian constraints. No doubt some such difference between Mapple's outlook and theirs is being insisted on. Nevertheless, a purely ideological reading of Mapple obscures the fact that he too in his imagination of a voyage offers answers to the set of questions Ishmael raises in "Loomings" and Ahab confronts in the hunt for Moby Dick.

Above all, Melville has Mapple preach his sermon in a setting that massively suggests how New England seaboard Calvinism deals with death and the fear of death. When Ishmael enters the chapel, it seems that he has inadvertently found his way into a coffin warehouse. He is surrounded not only by memorials to the dead but also by the "insular" and "silent grief" of widows and sailors bereaved of their mates and loved ones (Chap. 7). Like the chameleon he is, Ishmael adapts to the setting, tries for the moment to find common ground with the mourners, and gives Mapple a due hearing. Mapple uses the Jonah story to instruct his "shipmates" how to lead their lives in the face of temptation so as to die a sanctified death. Jonah's ordeal once past, he becomes a Protestant saint who lives in grace and dies in glory.

Of course, Mapple palpably misreads his biblical text by presenting the restored Jonah as God's repentant servant preaching "Truth to the face of Falsehood" (Chap. 9) and by ignoring the narrow-minded restored Jonah of Scripture who quarrels with God's message of mercy to Nineveh. By involving Mapple in this misreading, Melville undercuts Mapple's claim to authority and invites the reader to view Mapple's Christianity ironically. Like all versions of the voyage elaborated earlier or later, Mapple's version is particular to him and partial in its perspective. He reads Jonah's encounter with the wild unknown as a particular Calvinist-trained New Englander. In some ways Mapple contemplates Melville's sea as will Ahab, another product of the same religious culture; the two figures are linked imaginatively as well as divided. Ahab is as scornful of mere worldly power as any Quaker or Puritan. He too "against the proud gods and commodores of this earth, ever stands forth his own inexorable self." Like Mapple, Ahab imagines the whale and the sea as dreadful creations of God. Ahab's God is as fierce as Mapple's; yet Ahab declares war on his God, whereas Mapple worships his with the reverence due the mysterious, punishing power underlying all life. By a discipline of prayer and repentance, of self-denial to the world and self-assertion on God's behalf, the saint reenacts the prescribed Calvinist voyage through tempests to bliss.

The reward of such discipline is that Jonah and the saints fulfill "the chief end of man," which in the words of the Shorter Catechism is "to glorify God, and to enjoy him forever."[8] At the end of his sermon, Mapple modulates into an Edwardsean rapture over the endless enjoyments of the Christian voyager. "Delight, — topgallant delight is to him, who acknowledges no law or lord, but the Lord his God, and is only a patriot to heaven. . . . And eternal delight and deliciousness will be his, who coming to lay him down, can say with his final breath — O Father! — chiefly known to me by Thy rod – mortal or immortal, here I die. I have striven to be Thine, more than to be this world's, or mine own. Yet this is nothing; I leave eternity to Thee; for what is man that he should live out the lifetime of his God?'' (Chap. 9). Mapple may not believe with Queequeg that "the stars are isles," but his mariner has a similar assurance of comfort in the face of death. He gladly relinquishes the search for meaning, since God is unknowable, but his faith offers a framework for imagining how to struggle right-eously in a wild and mysterious universe, a ringed horizon full of human falsehood and natural evil.

It is a sign of Melville's capacious understanding that he repre-sents Mapple sympathetically as well as critically. Mapple's vision-ary Calvinism brings sweetness and hope to his parishioners even while his strenuous piety imparts a gloomy discipline to their lives. Slightly later in the story, the Nantucket Quaker Captain Bildad evinces a similar combination of dismal morality and hopeful imagination. Though Mapple and Bildad attend different church-es, they represent virtually the same ideology in the novel. At least when Bildad pilots the *Pequod* out of the Nantucket harbor in "Merry Christmas," he seems an extension of Mapple's spirit among the heathen and the reprobate. He comforts himself at the sight of the sea by chanting a hymn that calls up a vision of a Christian voyage to a happy eternity. Yet the context in which the hymn appears makes it clear that other members of the crew con-strue their voyages differently from Bildad. The narrative here is a concise demonstration of the multiple possibilities of voyaging. The sailors manning the windlass have a different idea from Bildad of what constitutes happiness. "Bildad . . . might now be seen . . . at intervals singing what seemed a dismal stave of psalmody, to cheer the hands at the windlass, who roared forth some sort of chorus about the girls in Booble Alley, with hearty good will" (Chap. 22). The sailors think to find their delight and deliciousness in Booble Alley, a squalid street in Liverpool's red-light district. Meanwhile, Bildad stays blithely and dismally oblivious to their profanity. Up to this point Bildad is only a comic figure, still a caricature of the tight-fisted Quaker. Yet, as he sings, he discloses more intimate longings typical of the Christian wayfarer. He too has a version of the voyage to communicate.

Lank Bildad, as pilot, headed the first watch, and ever and anon, as the old craft deep dived into the green seas, and sent the shivering frost all over her, and the winds howled, and the cordage rang, his steady notes were heard, —

> "Sweet fields beyond the swelling flood,
>   Stand dressed in living green.
> So to the Jews old Canaan stood,
>   While Jordan rolled between."

Never did those sweet words sound more sweetly to me than then. They were full of hope and fruition. Spite of this frigid winter night in the boisterous Atlantic, spite of my wet feet and wetter jacket, there was yet, it then seemed to me, many a pleasant haven in store; and meads and glades so eternally vernal, that the grass shot up by the spring, untrodden, unwilted, remains at midsummer. (Chap. 22)

Bildad has his inward eye on Mapple's heaven. The words he recalls are from Isaac Watts's well-known hymn, "There Is a Land of Pure Delight."[9] Through his Christian imagination, the death-dealing green seas are transformed into the "living green" of fields beyond the flood. For the moment, the reader is wholly taken with these Christian images and shares in Bildad's vision of heaven, as later he or she will share in Queequeg's. Yet Ishmael's reaction distorts Bildad's meaning and ensures that the reader's infatuation will be fluid and temporary. Ishmael's own image of "meads and glades eternally vernal" is secular and poetic rather than biblical. His vision of spring grass flourishing unchanged through the seasons recalls Blake's evocation of Beulah in *Milton*, or Thoreau's emblem of rambling "into higher and higher grass" at the end of *Walden*, or Whitman's celebration of grass on "a transparent summer morning" in "Song of Myself"[10] — all romantic transmutations of the Protestant sweet fields of Eden or Canaan. Like these writers, Ishmael uses his Protestant nurturing to feed his imagination of a natural paradise. Thus, in this brief passage, as in *Moby-Dick* as a whole, different shipmates are on different voyages. As they contemplate putting out to sea, ordinary tars remember Booble Alley, Bildad the land of Canaan, and Ishmael a redeemed meadow out of Whitman, whereas the *Pequod* itself travels through the icy waves to its unknown destiny. Melville does not choose between these images, but offers them all as alternative conceptions of voyaging on his wonder-freighted, murderous sea.

The hands at the windlass roaring forth a profane chorus are no visionaries like Bildad or Ishmael. Yet the voyage of all the book's visionaries is sustained and ballasted by the more mundane voyage of the crew. Since so much of the book is concerned with ordinary whaling rather than with the search for Moby Dick, the attitudes and activities of the crew bulk large in the narrative. True, this is no ordinary crew as Melville imagines it, but a set of isolated strangers with idiosyncratic temperaments cast together on a common mission. "They were nearly all . . . *Isolatoes* . . . not acknowledging the common continent of men, but each *Isolato* living on a separate continent of his own. Yet now, federated along one keel, what a set these Isolatoes were! An Anacharsis Clootz deputation from all the isles of the sea, and all the ends of the earth, accompanying Old Ahab in the Pequod to lay the world's grievances before that bar from which not very many of them ever came back" (Chap. 27). Such a speculation suggests that each sailor has a voyage of his own to travel, as is borne out in Melville's individual treatments of Pip or Queequeg or the Blacksmith or the Manxman. Also, the passage links the crew in spirit to Ahab even before he has them take the oath of vengeance against the White Whale. They too have a grievance against some unnamed injustice, much as Clootz's deputation to the French National Assembly shared a grievance against the world's ruling classes. We will see how their inclination toward vengeance partly causes their demise. Yet at times the crew is treated not so much as a collection of Isolatoes as a single massed group "federated along one keel"; and this massed group is given a character distinct from Ahab's or from that of any of the more introspective voyagers on board. At such times the common impulse that drives them is both simpler and more frightening than what motivates an Ishmael or a Starbuck.

When Ishmael first enters the Spouter Inn in New Bedford, on one wall of the entry he sees a display of murder weapons used in whaling, "a heathenish array of monstrous clubs and spears. Some were thickly set with glittering teeth resembling ivory saws; others were tufted with knots of human hair; and one was sickle-shaped, with a vast handle sweeping round like the segment made in the new-mown grass by a long-armed mower" (Chap. 3). Such a display is a memorial to "the honor and glory of whaling" (Chap. 82), a celebration of the savagery of the hunt. The impression Ishmael takes in is of reckless, primitive power, an impression complicated but not effaced by his later sights of sailors on shore – as when he sees "a wild set of mariners" (Chap. 3) from the crew of the *Grampus* who trample into the inn noisily at night, then sit silent like "bashful bears" at breakfast the next morning while Queequeg grapples rare beefsteaks toward him with his harpoon (Chap. 5). This is a variegated world of masculine power barely restrained by Presbyterianism.

Sailors, Ishmael remarks later, are savages. "Your true whale-hunter is as much a savage as an Iroquois" (Chap. 57). The whaleman's "long exile from Christendom" makes possible his zest not only for the hunt but for all uncivilized sensual enjoyments. When the crew or the harpooners take center stage, the text often expresses a great release of libido, in scenes of eating and drinking and touching on shore or at sea or of communal butchery in the whaleboats. This wish for release from restrictiveness is one reason for the general voyage. Much of the book's humor accompanies the release, as in Stubb's humorous monologues to his boat crew or Ishmael's indecorous verbal play with the bodies of whales and men in the cetological chapters. The feeling of liberation that comes with killing and other savage enjoyments is also associated with American independence, as in the episode from "Pitchpoling" when Stubb hurls his lance at the whale:

> Next moment with a rapid, nameless impulse, in a superb lofty arch the bright steel spans the foaming distance, and quivers in the life spot of the whale. Instead of sparkling water, he now spouts red blood.
> "That drove the spigot out of him!" cries Stubb. " 'Tis July's immortal Fourth; all fountains must run wine to-day! Would now, it were old Orleans whiskey, or old Ohio, or unspeakable old Monongehela!" (Chap. 84)

Hunting, whiskey, and freedom – these bring happiness to the American savage; these epitomize what he seeks on his voyage. Melville does not simply condemn this. "What is called savagery"

46

is after all "that condition in which God placed" mankind (Chap. 57). Melville may well have felt that he had "written a wicked book"[11] partly because in it he gave such free rein to masculine desire. Yet in "Pitchpoling" he also makes Stubb's pleasure in murder disquieting. With Ishamel, the reader participates in it ambivalently, with an answering pleasure in Stubb's skill and wit, but also with moral sense outraged.

What such a scene suggests – and there are several similar ones in the middle portion of the book from "Stubb Kills a Whale" to "The Grand Armada" – is that man in his natural savagery exists in a condition of enmity with nature. The savage whaleman loves the beauty of the Pacific but is also aware of "the tiger heart that pants beneath" the sea's lovely surface (Chap. 114). When Ishmael calls attention to both the sea's loveliness and its cannibalism, he not only speaks for himself but also articulates the unconscious common moral and aesthetic sense of all whalemen. But distinctly from him, their natural human way of dealing with the violence and death and apparent meaninglessness in nature, I surmise, is to become killers themselves. One ought perhaps to exempt Queequeg, "the well-governed shark,"[12] from the charge of human murderousness insofar as his tribal wisdom restrains him from indiscriminate violence; yet as part of Ahab's crew, he joins Flask and Tashtego and the rest in their voyage of vindictiveness. The crew's enmity against whales is emblematic of their unconscious grievance against the world given them, and this grievance is the hypo that attracts them to crazy Ahab. To put it this baldly may be presumptuous. When Ishmael wonders what makes the crew so eager to hunt Moby Dick, he puts his own surmise more tentatively. "What the White Whale was to them, or how to their unconscious understandings, also, in some dim, unsuspected way, he might have seemed the gliding great demon of the seas of life, – all this to explain, would be to dive deeper than Ishmael can go" (Chap. 41). Yet the idea he plants so questioningly is the same: Natural man has a common gliding demon enemy in nature. It takes little persuasion for Ahab to convince the crew that the White Whale embodies all that they naturally fear and hate.

This enmity is splendidly realized dramatically in the last fatal

47

gesture by a member of the crew at the end of their failed chase. When Tashtego hammers the sky-hawk's wing to the mainmast as the *Pequod* goes down, each stroke of the hammer releases his vitality and hate. Somehow Melville makes the reader cheer for Tashtego at this moment. In spirit we join him in his vindictive violence against "the bird of heaven" (Chap. 135). Yet perhaps only with a more savage part of our minds – because we also sense that he has his fate coming to him. On a subliminal level, the destruction of the *Pequod* is made to seem an appropriate reward not just for Ahab's vengeful pride but also for the crew's unbridled desire in their pursuit of the whale throughout the book.

So the quest ends in disaster. The *Pequod* and its crew "sink to hell" with Ahab (Chap. 135). If such a phrase is perhaps a rhetorical flourish, the voyage is nonetheless tragic and fatal for all these Isolatoes. Each disappears bearing with him his particular aspiration, his rendering of the world's text. Pip and Queequeg may find peace in their separate heavens, as the book elsewhere hints, but even they die unknowable deaths in the remorseless sea.

Only Ishmael survives. His survival may be a modest cause for hope, or just an accident, or both. Melville leaves it ambiguous as to whether he survives because of his superior virtue. He is both morally involved in the doomed crew and set apart from it in the story. Even in the first chapter he is both a common sailor and a reflective loner. On the *Pequod* he joins his shipmates in their pleasures and aspirations, but also separates himself from them. He shares in their work and recreation, never missing a chance for carousing even after he leaves the ship. At the same time, his narrative of bloodthirsty scenes in the middle of the book shows repeatedly that he can learn compassion for the whale from observing his murder by man. And he appears to renounce Ahab's feud before the final chase. There are hints in "The Grand Armada" and "A Squeeze of the Hand" that like the Ancient Mariner he eventually learns to love "all things both great and small."[13] Yet Melville does not make his meaning as transparent as such hints might suggest. Ishmael's peculiar narrative function itself makes the meaning of his survival uncertain.

As narrator of a multiple quest, Ishmael is implicated in all the other voyagers. He participates in their imaginations; their different renderings of the voyage are part of what he learns in his own search for knowledge. As I have said, he is a chameleon of a narrator. Successively he takes on the coloration of a Father Mapple, a Queequeg, an Ahab, or a Stubb. As such, he is the right recording angel for the many possibilities of the soul these characters represent. Moreover, his shiftiness as a narrator in telling their different stories consorts well with the fluid consciousness he exhibits in the essayistic chapters, where he seems often to speak with the voice of Herman Melville — though Melville does not share his narrator's limitations, or indeed his dramatic opportunities. From his role as a chameleon narrator-character, Ishmael extracts moral benefits but also suffers moral disabilities. He knows everything that all the characters know and can reflect on it. He can take multiple perspectives on "God, the Devil, & Life," never falling into the trap of giving universal applications to temporary opinions. He even grows wiser in the course of the voyage. Because he loves Queequeg, he can share Queequeg's sense of peace with the world and participate at least once in his inscrutable understanding of the prospect of death. Because he distances himself through pity from the crew and from Ahab, he can also maintain his distance from their predatory feuds. And yet not wholly. As their narrative vehicle, they continue to be part of him even after he has apparently renounced them. Functionally, it is impossible for him to take an active stand against them. Indeed, through him the reader learns to appreciate them and identify with them, with Ahab brooding on his vengeance, the crew glorying in the kill, and Tashtego hammering at the bird of heaven. But the result for Ishmael is that he is a passive, shifty, elusive character, with moments of moral virtue that disappear into the flow of his consciousness. He learns from his multiple perspectives to be not only a moralist but also an ironist whose irony incapacitates him for action. Aware of the possible meaninglessness of his aggregate of perspectives, he takes refuge in ironic loquaciousness. One feels this especially in the post-*Pequod* Ishmael of "The Town-Ho Story," where he is a giddy humorist telling tales of Moby Dick over and over, like an Ancient Mariner without the burdens of age and Christianity. Ishmael is no hero. Yet one implication of my approach is that *Moby-Dick* has no single hero. Ishmael at least is a visionary survivor, which may be all one can ask for on this frightening sea.

Melville, I believe, was intuitively aware of Ishmael's drawbacks and possibilities, for he splendidly sustains his ambiguous characterization of him in the Epilogue. It seems that Melville did not want his book to be comfortably resolved. He kept it fluid right through the closure he gave it. No single interpretation of the Epilogue can stand on its own, while several are still in play by the time we stop reading. Ishmael continues to have several roles even when he has no shipmates to project himself on imaginatively. These diverse roles, however, aptly epitomize the diverse sides of his character in the book as a whole. First, as he has been an insignificant and passive member of the crew, he is a mere chance fugitive from the wreck of the *Pequod*, owing his survival to "the Fates." "It so chanced, that . . . I was he whom the Fates ordained to take the place of Ahab's bowsman" (Epilogue). Presumably, the Fates let him live not for his good works or virtuous attitudes but because they have capriciously ordained that the "whaling voyage of one Ishmael" (Chap. 1) would end thus. Second, as Ishmael has been, significantly, a lover of Queequeg and of natural beauty, he survives at the end through friendship and natural magic. He grabs hold of Queequeg's coffin-canoe and floats miraculously to safety past sharks and sea-hawks. He thus renews his bosom friendship with Queequeg even after Queequeg takes his last long dive. The canoe, covered with a "mystical treatise on the art of attaining truth" (Chap. 110) that Ishmael cannot read even as he embraces it, is Queequeg's last gift to him. Ishmael is saved by love and mysterious knowledge. Third, as he has so often witnessed human and natural destructiveness, he survives as the witness of a disaster. In the epigram to the Epilogue, he likens himself to the messengers to Job, each of whom ends his report of Job's disasters with the words "And I only am escaped alone to tell thee" (Epilogue). As messenger he does not act, has no positive character. Yet as the teller of the tragic saga of the *Pequod*, Ishmael is potentially a tragic and ironic artist who can pitch his story to the reader-as-Job, the reader who should by now be aware that man's aspirations for knowledge bring misery as well as wonder.

One can cajole these three roles into some sort of logical connection if one wishes, but I prefer not to. Instead, in my view, Ishmael remains Protean, in keeping with his Protean nature as narrator of a multiple quest. This is possible because he develops in the course of the voyage not only from an innocent greenhorn into a wise ex-whaleman but also from a mere character into a consciousness who can reach out to his fellows in reflective isolation. As a consciousness he survives to narrate *Moby-Dick* – in isolation. He has only the memory of friendship, and no more company than a fugitive from strangeness, wildness, meaninglessness, and an encounter with death on the Pacific can have. No wonder his final appearance is as "another orphan."

NOTES

1. Nathaniel Hawthorne, *The English Notebooks,* ed. Randall Stewart (New York: Modern Language Association of America, 1941), p. 433.
2. Quoted in Warner Berthoff, *The Example of Melville* (Princeton, N.J.: Princeton University Press, 1962), p. 24.
3. *The Complete Works of Ralph Waldo Emerson,* 12 vols., Centenary Edition, ed. E. W. Emerson (Boston: Houghton Mifflin, 1903), vol. 1, p. 76; vol. 2, p. 306.
4. From Melville's letters to Hawthorne of June 1 and November 17, 1851, as transcribed in Herman Melville, *Moby-Dick,* ed. Harrison Hayford and Hershel Parker (New York: Norton Critical Edition, 1967), pp. 560 and 566.
5. Cited in the Norton *Moby-Dick,* p. 613.
6. Harold Bloom, "The Internalization of Quest-Romance," rpt. in *Romanticism and Consciousness: Essays in Criticism,* ed. Harold Bloom (New York: Norton, 1970), pp. 3–24.
7. See Sacvan Bercovitch's interpretation of Cotton Mather's "*Nehemias Americanus:* The Life of John Winthrop," in *The Puritan Origins of the American Self* (New Haven, Conn.: Yale University Press, 1975), chap. 1 and passim.
8. *The Confession of Faith, the Larger and Shorter Catechisms, with the Scripture Proofs at Large, Together with the Sum of Saving Knowledge* (1958: rpt. London: Wickliffe Press of the Protestant Truth Society, 1962), p. 287.
9. Isaac Watts, *Psalms, Hymns, and Spiritual Songs,* ed. James M. Win-

chell (Boston: Lincoln & Edmonds, 1821), Hymn 626, n.p. Melville may well have known that this hymn bears the sententious title "A Prospect of Heaven Makes Death Easy." If so, his recollection of the stanza is probably tinged with irony as well as nostalgia.

10. William Blake, *Milton: Book the Second,* Plates 30 and 31, reprinted in *The Poetry and Prose of William Blake,* ed. David V. Erdman (Garden City, N.Y.: Doubleday, 1965), pp. 128–30. Henry D. Thoreau, *Walden* (Princeton, N.J.: Princeton University Press, 1971), p. 319. Walt Whitman, *Leaves of Grass: The First (1855) Edition,* ed. Malcolm Cowley (New York: The Viking Press, 1959), p. 28.

11. From Melville's November 17, 1851, letter to Hawthorne, as cited in the Norton *Moby-Dick,* p. 566.

12. Robert Zoellner, *The Salt-Sea Mastodon: A Reading of Moby-Dick* (Berkeley and Los Angeles: University of California Press, 1973), p. 215.

13. Samuel Taylor Coleridge, "The Rime of the Ancient Mariner," line 615, in *The Portable Coleridge,* ed. I. A. Richards (New York: Penguin, 1977), p. 104.

3

Moby-Dick as Sacred Text

LAWRENCE BUELL

MY title proposes an analogy rather than a definition. Clearly, *Moby-Dick* belongs to other genres as well. Tragedy, comedy, chronicle, epic – these and many more have been proposed, and can be made to stick. Melville's masterpiece also obviously lacks some of the distinguishing traits of scripture. No community of devotees has ever received it as a spiritual authority, nor was that Melville's intent, though he did like to think of his vocation as truth telling rather than tale telling.[1] Indeed, Melville's motives as a writer seem positively commercial compared with those of, say, Milton and Blake, both of whom claimed to write from divine dictation. And even if Melville himself had made such a claim, we might justly be skeptical. If "God chooses Milton to create a new scripture," asks one Miltonist shrewdly, "why must this scripture take the form of an epic poem? Are not the expectations created by the genre in conflict with the intentions of a sacred text?"[2] The same could be said with even greater force of a rambling jocular-serious narrative of a "WHALING VOYAGE BY ONE ISHMAEL" (Chap. 1).

Yet in certain ways *Moby-Dick is* a sort of scripture. It is, to begin with, indisputably one of the works of the American literary "canon," as scholars like to call it, read and taught by the professorial priesthood with a more genuinely religious zeal than most of that priesthood probably feel toward the literal sacred texts of their own ethnic traditions – the Torah, the New Testament, or whatever. In my field, to write a commentary on *Moby-Dick* is more respectable than to write a commentary on the book of Job or Jonah. One reason for this is the depth of the waters in which Melville fished, the fact that this particular fish story becomes ultimately in some sense a record of an encounter with the divine. The book's language is drenched in sacramentalism, "brimming over with signals of the transcendent."[3] When the white whale rises out of the water on the first day of the chase, it does not merely breach: "the grand god revealed himself" (Chap. 133). Here and at innumerable other points metaphor seems to convert story into myth.

"Despite all the heterodoxy of opinion on *Moby-Dick*, few critics doubt that Moby Dick is a god."[4] Taken literally, that critical statement seems bizarre, especially in light of studies, during the two decades since it was made, that have placed much emphasis on how the world of *Moby-Dick* communicates to the reader through the filter of "Ishmael's quandaries as both neophyte whaleman and retrospective narrator" as to "whether the White Whale is simply a naturalistic whale or whether he is a creature of supernatural properties."[5] The book can even be read as a gigantic spoof of the sacred imagination from animism (Ishmael measuring the whale's skeleton in the Arsacides in the face of horrified priestly opposition) to the Bible itself (the credibility of the Book of Jonah uproariously sabotaged in Chapter 83 under the guise of defense). T. Walter Herbert, elsewhere in this volume, shows in detail how *Moby-Dick* critiques both the orthodox and liberal sectarianisms of Melville's day, particularly the former. So suffused with indeterminacy and satire is the book that to read it simply as a work of prophetic witness would be to commit an oversimplification parallel to Ahab's oversimplification of the meaning of the voyage. Yet as Herbert also attests, the sense of the sacred with which the world of the book and particularly the figure of the white whale are infused never evaporates, but on the contrary continues to be resuggested even as it is questioned, so that H. Bruce Franklin is quite right in affirming that "the wild mythmaking of the sea attains the highest seriousness, and ridicule is reserved for the particular myths of the world's lands."[6] Indeed, it is possible to argue that this element of "ridicule" itself falls at least partially within the bounds of the sacred imagination. Take, for instance, the fourth and final chapter of the Book of Jonah, a dialogue between the solicitious but urbanely condescending voice of God and the alienated prophet, who is sulking because God has elected

not to destroy the repentant Ninevites after chastising the disobe-
dient Jonah into obeying the divine order to warn them of their
impending doom. This scene is a comic counterpart to the much
more famous Jonah-and-the-whale sequence. Both dramatize the
incomprehension and resistance of God's ways to be found even
(and in this case especially) among God's appointed messengers,
the first two chapters doing so on a level of high seriousness, the
last on the level of comic anecdote, as Jonah pouts with absurd
self-importance by his withered gourd vine.

Any attempt to understand how the sense of the sacred is dealt
with in *Moby-Dick* is thus a tricky business. *Moby-Dick* becomes a
sort of modern Book of Revelation, yet also a book that casts doubt
on the possibility of revelation, yet again in that very act of doubt-
casting a work that stands not firmly opposed to sacred literary
tradition but remains in some measure faithful to a biblical sense
of God's elusiveness of human conception. The purpose of this
essay is to suggest more specifically how *Moby-Dick* should be read
in light of these complications, first by putting Melville briefly in
historical perspective, then by providing more detailed examination of some aspects of the style and structure of Melville's
masterpiece.[7]

1

One of the major intellectual forces behind the whole so-called
American literary renaissance to which Melville's work contributed was a religious ferment and anxiety resulting from the breakdown of consensual dogmatic structures and particularly the
breakdown of biblical authority in Protestant America.[8] This had
both "negative" and "positive" aspects. Negatively, the rise of the
"higher criticism" in biblical studies, which began to make significant inroads in America during the decade of Melville's birth,
seemed threatening and destructive in its approach to the Bible
(and, by extension, to institutionalized Christianity as a whole) as
a culture-bound, historical artifact subject to the same methods of
interpretation and susceptible to the same errors and obsolescence
as any other ancient artifact. This threatened to reduce holy scripture to myth in the bad sense – to quaint superstitious fabrication.

Concomitantly, however, a less parochial and more creative understanding of the religious imagination now became possible, an affirmative reading of myth as the expression of spiritual archetypes informing not only the Bible but the scriptures of all cultures, and not only ancient texts but – at least potentially – the literature of one's own day as well. At least partially offsetting the disillusioning sense that prophets were no more than poets was the exciting dream that poets might be prophets. This indeed was one of the great themes of the romantic movement in both England and America. It was wholly in keeping with this thrust of romanticism that its first major American exemplar, Ralph Waldo Emerson, was an ex-minister who, in reaction against contemporary theology and denominationalism, turned to the vocation of freelance lecturer-writer, defining it as a secular priesthood. Emerson's scattered comments bearing on the relation between poetry and prophecy provide the best American statement of how the demythologizing of Judeo-Christianity could give rise to creative remythologizing as well as to simple negation.

The most convenient starting place for inquiry into this aspect of Emersonianism is his 1838 graduation *Address* to the senior class of divinity students at Harvard. Although we cannot be certain whether Melville ever read this address, let alone whether it influenced him,[9] it is nonetheless valuable for Melvilleans for its quite explicit presentation of what might be called the orthodox American high romantic view of the relation between scripture and poesis, within and against which other writers of the period formed their own positions.

Emerson's fundamental argument is simple: The acceptance of Jesus's authority over us, on which institutionalized Christianity is based, represents a false crystallization of Jesus's figurative speech ("this high chant from the poet's lips"), the true intent of which was not merely to say "I am divine" but that "God incarnates himself in man, and evermore goes forth anew to take possession of his world." Hence "Christianity became a Mythus, as the poetic teaching of Greece and of Egypt, before." To be true to the prophetic message that institutionalization has occluded, the preacher of today must therefore not be a custodian but a "bard of the Holy

Ghost" who, through his own prophetic utterance, will "acquaint men at first hand with Deity." "I look," concludes Emerson,

> for the hour when that supreme Beauty, which ravished the souls of those Eastern men, and chiefly of those Hebrews, and through their lips spoke oracles to all time, shall speak in the West also.

He looks, indeed, for nothing less than the completion of the as yet fragmentary Bible.

> The Hebrew and Greek Scriptures contain immortal sentences, that have been bread of life to millions. But they have no epical integrity; are fragmentary; are not shown in their order to the intellect. I look for the new Teacher, that shall follow so far those shining laws, that he shall see them come full circle; shall see their rounding complete grace . . . [10]

Emerson's approach, in short, is first to call for demythologizing, then for remythologizing; first to dismantle the edifice believed to be complete, then to urge its completion from what is now seen to be fragments. The ground of appeal is in each case the access that every age has to divinely inspired poetic vision. That, as Emerson sees it, is Jesus's core message. That message, as Emerson interprets it, both gives the lie to any attempt to claim authoritativeness for a single prophet and creates the opportunity for genuine prophecy in the present. The sermon is aimed, of course, at ministers rather than at creative writers. But the link between prophecy and poesis is constant throughout Emerson's work. Literature and scripture become interchangeable categories. Scripture is to be understood as creative art, and what differentiates enduring art from competent workmanship is its prophetic dimension.

Emerson's dream that today's verbal artists, be they preachers or poets, might speak with prophetic authority was powerfully appealing to his age as a whole, which saw the production of at least one new Bible (*The Book of Mormon*) and two epoch-making literary works that laid direct claim to divine inspiration: Harriet Beecher Stowe's *Uncle Tom's Cabin* and Walt Whitman's *Leaves of Grass*. Melville's writing clearly also reflects this dream both in taking aim at the theological status quo and in using fiction (and later poetry) as vehicles for reflecting on the range of ultimate questions with which the Bible itself is preoccupied.

Two points, however, differentiate Emerson's notion of literary scripturism from Melville's. First, Emerson's remains more Christocentric. In the Divinity School *Address* he advises the fledgling preachers to "let the breath of new life be breathed by you through the forms already existing";[11] he rejects Jesus as an authority partly on the authority of Jesus himself; and he urges a completion rather than a replacement of "The Hebrew and Greek Scriptures." Emerson proposes here, in other words, a new hermeneutic or school of interpretation as much as a new Gospel.[12] This proposal is partly strategic, an adaptation of his rhetoric to the particular audience. Some other Emerson works, such as the poems "Brahma" and "The World Soul," adopt a more resolutely dechristianized frame of reference. Still, it is not until the second generation of American romantics that the religious imagination really begins to pull away from its Judeo-Christian and specifically Protestant roots, and we find Thoreau claiming that oriental faiths appeal more to him than his forefathers; Whitman equating Jehovah with "old Brahm" and "Saturnius" as he chants the "square" (*not* "trinity"!) "deific"; and Melville purporting to see the worship of Yojo and Jehovah (semihomonyms by no accident) as interchangeable rituals. Melville indeed goes much further than this, appropriating for symbolic purposes the imagery and vocabularies of all major and selected "primitive" world religions. In Emersonian transcendentalism, we see the birth of comparative religion as a discipline and as a literary force; in *Moby-Dick* we see something like a full literary efflorescence, well ahead of its progress as a field of academic inquiry, which blossomed only in the late nineteenth century.[13]

Second, Emerson's *Address,* although more restrained and refined than Melvillean narrative style, is also more authoritarian. Emerson lays down his new law and then looks forward to "the new Teacher" who will articulate it fully, thereby in effect imposing a new era of "secondhand revelations," as a recent critic astutely points out.[14] Due in part, but only in part, to the greater circuitousness of narrative as against expository form, Melville's rhetoric increasingly lacks such assurance. Emerson himself became more cautious and hedging as he entered his forties, indeed notorious for evasion and multiplicity; but even the late Emerson can be counted on to fall back at some point on a slightly modified set of core doctrines. Melville might be said to have pushed to an extreme limit the invitation Emerson extends at his most open-ended: that we speak our mind without regard for consistency or closure. *Moby-Dick*'s short, autonomous chapters are the narrative equivalent of Emerson's semidetached passages: Each is a new stab at truth, often from a different vantage point. Except that whereas Emerson, for the most part, spins his pinwheel confidently, assured that the universe coheres even if his essay doesn't, Melville wonders if the chase has any meaning at all beyond what we project upon it. So the elder romantic finally presents us with an aesthetics of faith, the younger with an aesthetics of doubt.

2

But it is high time to look at Melville more closely. His general orientation is aptly characterized by Robert Richardson as "mythic investiture": the infusion of what we know to be natural phenomena with a sense of mystic otherness. "Although we never lose sight of the fact that Moby Dick is simply a large albino sperm whale, it is, from the start, the *idea* of the great whale that compels us as it compels Ishmael. . . . We see the whale through a veil of rumor, scholarship, legend, and myth; by imperceptible degrees we come to acquiesce in the appropriateness of such things, and we eventually find ourselves regarding the whale as something more than a whale."[15] Richardson's "simply" strikes me as narrowing the range of options the text keeps open, but otherwise this is an admirable summation. What is especially interesting and distinctive about the investiture process is how the narrative builds this impression in the face of the narrator's disclaimers and even discreditation. A convenient example is Chapter 86, "The Tail," convenient for being an almost paradigmatic illustration of how the cetology chapters in general work. All interweave most of the following elements:

1. A substratum of cetological data, testifying to the American – and Melvillean – passion for "informative" unfamiliar lore

("the compact round body of its root expands into two broad, firm, flat palms or flukes").

2. Rhetorical intensification of the data ("Could annihilation occur to matter, this were the thing to do it").

3. Metaphorization of the data, so as to begin to dissolve the shipboard context (a series of comparisons between the whale's tail and the elephant's trunk).

4. Mythification of the data ("Out of the bottomless profundities the gigantic tail seems spasmodically snatching at the highest heaven. So in dreams, have I seen majestic Satan thrusting forth his tormented colossal claw from the flame Baltic of Hell").

5. Complication of the mythic framework so as to introduce the possibility of solipsism ("But in gazing at such scenes, it is all in all what mood you are in; if in the Dantean, the devils will occur to you; if in that of Isaiah, the archangels").

6. Comic disruption of the mythic framework (the tongue-in-cheek image of whales "praying" with peaked flukes like "the military elephants of antiquity" that, according to Ishmael's source, "often hailed the morning with their trunks uplifted in the profoundest silence").

7. Self-conscious proclamation of scribal inadequacy ("The more I consider this mighty tail, the more do I deplore my inability to express it").

8. Ambiguous reformulation of the whale as mystery ("Dissect him how I may, then, I but go skin deep; I know him not, and never will. But if I know not even the tail of this whale, how understand his head? much more, how comprehend his face, when he has none? Thou shalt see my back parts, my tail, he seems to say, but my face shall not be seen. But I cannot completely make out his back parts; and hint what he will about his face, I say again he has no face").

This last gesture, with which the chapter ends, is particularly suggestive. It teeters on the edge of comic absurdity, with the (deliberately?) lame puns "I go but skin deep" and "the tail of this whale," and with the (whimsically? mischievously?) hyperbolic appropriation of Yahweh's warning to Moses on Horeb (Exodus 34:23): "thou shalt see my back parts: but my face shall not be seen" (King James version). Yet coming on top of Satan, the archangels, and so forth, and in the context of practical documentation of the whale's power and inscrutability, the gesture of divination also makes dramatic sense. To the extent that we hear the former note, we shall read the passage and Ishmael's discourses generally as testifying to the quixoticism of the myth-making process; and we shall want to ascribe to Melville or at least to Ishmael the debunking conception of myth as fabrication. This leads, on the level of symbol interpretation, to a reading of *Moby-Dick* as an allegory of reading and particularly as an allegory of unreadability: the undecipherability of the whale as text. Ishmael's account in "Cetology" of his enterprise as an incomplete "draught," classifying whales in terms of books, lends support to this interpretation, as does the pervasive hieroglyph imagery.[16] To the extent that we hear the latter note, we shall still read *Moby-Dick* as preoccupied with the whale's indecipherability, but we shall hesitate to suppose that the text therefore shows that mythicizations of the White Whale are nothing more than artifacts of the observer's desire (which is Ishmael's judgment on Ahab and Pip's judgment on the whole crew in Chapter 99, "The Doubloon"). In this case, we shall want to think, indeed, of the luminousness with which the mystery of Moby Dick has been invested as the heart of that which is undecipherable. This response leads ultimately to a reading of *Moby-Dick* as about an encounter with the realm of the transcendent that dramatizes parallel failures of human striving (Ahab) and knowing (Ishamel). In this reading, Ishmaelean mockery of the kind just noted starts to look like self-protective compensation for the frustration and anxiety of failing to grasp the elusive, mysterious, and therefore threatening Other. It is through the eyes of this second reading that *Moby-Dick* begins to look somewhat like a sacred text.

That this second reading is more persuasive as well as more powerful than the first is strongly suggested by the book's narrative structure. The narrative "proves" Ahab to have been a false prophet, but it does not disown the framework of supernaturalism established by his shadow Fedallah's three *Macbeth*-like prophecies, which uncannily come to pass. The narrative leaves open the question of whether the White Whale is a divine or demonic agent, and in leaving this question open leaves us in a state of wonder rather than with a confident reduction of the whale to the status of material object or (on the symbolic level) narcissistic projection. Particularly interesting in this regard is the first closeup of Moby Dick:

> Not the white bull Jupiter swimming away with ravished Europa clinging to his graceful horns; his lovely, leering eyes sideways intent upon the maid; with smooth bewitching fleetness, rippling straight for the nuptial bower in Crete; not Jove, not that great majesty Supreme! did surpass the glorified White Whale as he so divinely swam (Chap. 133)

Franklin rightly calls this "one of the great moments of revelation in literature."[17] Not that we should yield to the temptation of concluding "Aha! this *proves* that Melville thinks Moby Dick is a god – be he agent or principal." The passage doesn't quite do that. As an epic simile, it advertises itself as possibly "only" a literary device, as a device that beautifies rhetoric by infusing a dose of classical decor, thereby betraying consciousness of artifice in the midst of worshipful enthusiasm.[18] At the same time, the passage even more strenuously resists such reduction through its use of what might be called the grand Miltonic tradition of the negative classical simile for purposes of spiritual exaltation. When Milton describes Eden, he does so by singing how the fair fields of Enna, the Castalian Spring, the Isle of Nysa, and so forth cannot match it. For Wordsworth, in turn, neither Chaos nor "The darkest pit of lowest Erebus" "can breed such fear and awe/As fall upon us often when we look/Into our Minds, into the Mind of Man,/My haunt, and the main region of my Song."[19] Neither, likewise, is the White Whale to be surpassed by previous avatars of the ultimate. Negation in each case is a way of reaping the benefits of metaphorical analogizing while establishing that the subject at hand has an autonomous glory not preempted by any analogy in terms of which it might be seen. Later moments in the chase sequence call the whale-as-supreme-and-lovely-being passage into question, with suggestions that its intent might be malignant or haphazard. But the rhetoric of apocalypse is never revoked. At most, one could accuse Melville of temporizing in the quoted passage by establishing the whale's "great majesty Supreme" only in terms of a pagan analogue, by hesitating to analogize to Jehovah himself as Ishmael had done in "The Tail," as Wordsworth dared to do more solemnly in the Prospectus to *The Recluse*.[20]

The reader of *Moby-Dick* is all the more eager to experience the White Whale's appearance as apocalyptic after such long fore-shadowing — after hundreds of premonitory references to the "grand hooded phantom, like a snow hill in the air" (Chap. 1). Here the book plays an interesting double game. Because its central subject is an absent object of obsession for nearly the entire narrative, the text continually signals to the reader that "This is not yet quite reality; this is only preparatory information or interpretation." Not until a third of the book is over does an encounter with even an ordinary whale take place. During this long buildup, the repetitous quality of the cetology chapters and of Ishmael's meditations in general, combined with the fundamental fact of Moby Dick's absence, reinforce the plausibility of the frequent hints that the quest is empty of meaning except for what is read into it. On the basis of what we are allowed to see, nothing is easier than to subscribe to Ishmael's mock lament:

> How vain and foolish, then, thought I, for timid untravelled man to try to comprehend aright this wondrous whale, by merely poring over his dead attenuated skeleton. (Chap. 103)

— a complaint that applies both to the idolatrous devotion of the Arsacidean priests and to Ishmael's whole project of trying to construct a symbolic edifice from the whale's various body parts. Nothing is easier at this point than to accept Ishmael's revision of Ahab's reading of "The Whiteness of the Whale," according to which Ishmael does not precisely reject Ahab's theory of Moby Dick as malignant so much as reconceive his balefulness in terms of cosmic blankness or meaninglessness ("a colorless, all-color of atheism from which we shrink" [Chap. 42]), as opposed to purposive ill, thus depriving the sense of evil of any coherence or plan. At the same time, the plethora of foreshadowings and the repeated admissions of intellectual defeat and skepticism create intense frustration for the reader as well as the narrator (as every teacher of undergraduates knows) and with this a great longing for closure, which the text in the long run pretty much provides. Near the end, the narrative becomes much more linear; the whale's eruption into the text and disposal of the *Pequod* dissipates the haze of speculation in the sense of providing a resolution, at least on the plot level, to the prior state of indefiniteness. In this sense, Bainard Cowan is precisely right in claiming that "the final events of the book do away with ambiguity and determine all meaning toward one end."[21] The narrative structure is reminiscent of the tale of Job without the frame. In each work, redundant expostulation and soul searching build up to an intolerable pitch of uncertainty until abruptly resolved by authoritative, repressive intervention – except that in Melville the whale speaks only on the level of action.

In other words, Ishmael's speculations can never end; the book can never be more than "the draught of a draught" (Chap. 32); the inevitability of thematic nonresolution makes Ishmael's desire to keep his work unfinished a completely honest and proper stance; but the premonition/conjecture-to-manifestation pattern gives dramatic support to the passages that define the advent of the White Whale as an apocalypse. For dramatic reasons, it becomes impossible at the end to read the White Whale definitely as an empty sign or mere solipsistic construct. Any such emptiness becomes at least as plausibly explicable as a reflection of human inability to fathom the full meaning of the "noumenal epiphany" of Chapter 133, as Robert Zoellner calls it.[22] The apocalypse of the White Whale, both because of the mythicized imagery investing it and because of its dramatic position within the narrative, gives at least the appearance of substance to the void created by the speculations of both Ahab and Ishmael. Absence is replaced by plenitude – at least of a sort.

The status of what I have called the apocalypse of the White Whale can be clarified further with the aid of Paul Ricoeur's "Toward a Hermeneutic of the Idea of Revelation." As a textual phenomenon, revelation as Ricoeur sees it is not "a monolithic concept" but a "pluralistic" and "polysemic" compound of overlapping forms of discourse, of which Ricoeur defines five in his schematic classification: prophetic, narrative, prescriptive, wisdom, and hymnic. All five, I think, can be detected in *Moby-Dick*, but only the first two need concern us here. The mark of the first is "the idea of a double author of speech and writing. Revelation is the speech of another," that is, God, "behind the speech of the prophet."[23] In *Moby-Dick* Ahab's discourse claims the equivalent of this, but not Ishmael's. Ahab claims to speak as "the Fates' lieutenant" (Chap. 134). To be sure, his notion of "right worship" is "defiance" (Chap. 119), and in this he extends an occasional biblical trait of prophetic behavior (compare the will to deviance in Jeremiah and Jonah) and makes it his norm, arrogating prophetic power entirely to himself. What allows him to see his speech as having prophetic authority, however, is that his perceptions have a more than personal validity. On the Quarter-deck, for instance, he justifies pursuit of Moby Dick not merely for the sake of vengeance but because "Truth hath no confines" (Chap. 36). Vengeance must be justified in terms of some cosmic scheme. Ahab's "discourse of revelation," however, is of course made in the long run to seem a perversion of the real thing by being enclosed within Ishmael's, which makes no such pretense, even if at times it gestures faintly in that direction, as when Ishmael seriocomically announces his voyage as part of "the grand programme of Providence" (Chap. 1). Viewed as prophetic utterance, then, *Moby-Dick* presents a kind of antiscripture (Ahab's discourses) within a secularized and on the whole debunking commentary.

Conceived as revelation *narrative,* however, the scriptural status of *Moby-Dick* looks rather different. "What is essential in the case of narrative discourse," observes Ricoeur, "is the emphasis on the founding event or events as the imprint, mark, or trace of God's act. Confession takes place through narration, and the problematic of inspiration is in no way the primary consideration. God's mark is in history before being in speech. It is only secondarily in speech inasmuch as this history itself is brought to language in the speech-act of narration."[24] Insofar as the *Pequod's* encounter with the monster of the deep is a mysterious, deeply inexplicable, and magic-suggesting event that gives rise to the telling of the story in the first place and also, at the end of the tale, supersedes the telling in the sense that reflective commentary becomes largely displaced by the force of the narrative relation — insofar as all this is true, *Moby-Dick* begins to reemerge on the narrative level as sacred text even as it might have seemed that any pretenses to revelation had been contained by wily Ishmael. I take it that one of the reasons, maybe the main reason, for the inconsistency of Ishmael's disappearance from the later stages of the narrative may be to dramatize this very effect: the effect of what seems *comparatively* like a pure, unmediated vision of successive mysterious events bursting through the power of both commentary (Ishmael) and false prophecy (Ahab) to contain them. It is interesting in this regard that when Ishmael does reappear in the Epilogue, he seems to have been coopted by the discourse of revelation. He now speaks in the role of Job's messenger-servant, whose function is simply to serve as the reporter of the demonically arranged and divinely permitted catastrophe: "I only am escaped alone to tell thee" (Epilogue).

In retrospect, then, Ishmael's containment of Ahab's pseudo-prophetic pretensions is itself contained within the story of the *Pequod*'s encounter with the whale, the encounter that both gave rise to Ishmael's yarn and breaks through it to achieve something more closely approximating the discourse of revelation than that of Ishmael himself.[25] In retrospect, Ishmael's style of circumlocution can be seen both as a way of deferring and warding off the terror of the once-experienced encounter,[26] terrifying alike in its power and in its mysteriousness, and as a preparation for our also experiencing that encounter as powerful and mysterious. Ishmael appeals to experience as the proper test, corrective, and ground of human learning ("a whale-ship was my Yale College and my Harvard" [Chap. 24]), yet he must swim through libraries in order to tell his story – must swim through scores of Extracts in order even to get to his story. This learning immeasurably magnifies the proportions of the problem of the White Whale; but its paper speculations, in the face of the actual whale's ability to annihilate much solider wood products, are shown up as timorous, uninspired performances at last.

Numerous critics have noted that the use of dual foci in the novel – Ishmael the speculator and Ahab the actor – sets up a tension and a symbiosis between circular and linear thinking. Robert Caserio has extended this insight in a discerning analysis of Melvillean plotting that will be helpful here. "Melville dramatizes himself through Ishmael," notes Caserio, "as not actively telling or willfully writing his story and its ending. As an author and agent he, like his hero, wants to be seen as thrown clear of his work, as passive, himself at the mercy of the instability that 'features' event. This is his way of proving he is not the story's dictator, an Ahab-like sultanist of the brain."[27] The context of this observation is an extended analogy between Ahab as a representative of old-fashioned nineteenth-century realistic conceptions of linear plotting, and Melville through Ishmael as moving toward a modern form of open, circuitous, experimental, inconclusive plotting, which for Caserio correlates with a shift from activism to quietism in political ideology. I agree with most of this shrewd diagnosis but would qualify it by adding that Ishmael's abdication of authority and the text's ultimate suspension or at least minimization of Ishmael as a narrative presence may be seen as done not just in the interest of countering the Ahabian single vision but, beyond that, as a means of recovering at least the possibility of a providential event structure, which the text introduces when the White Whale swims apocalyptically into the book and brings it to an abrupt but tidy close at the narrative level. Just as Ahab's liberties with political authority must not go unchastised, so Ishmael's liberties as discursive narrator must be rectified by resort to a linear revelation narrative – a linear narrative, at any rate, that continues to hold forth the possibility that a more than merely literary revelation has taken place.

The prospect of the authority of revelation at the prophetic level, eroded by Ishmael's critique of Ahab, is thus partially recovered at the level of plot through the agency of the whale and through the move toward greater objectification of the narrative voice. The narrative method of having the tale eventually seem to reabsorb and outstrip its teller reflects and repeats the romantic impulse both to demythologize and remythologize. In this it reflects, but with a difference, Emerson's dictum to the newborn bards of the Holy Ghost to "cast behind you all conformity, and acquaint men at first hand with Deity." The *form* of this prescription is enacted faithfully in *Moby-Dick* by Ishmael's exposure of the arbitrariness of all particular readings of the divine (starting with the juxtaposition of Father Mapple-ism and Yojo worship as equivalent rituals) in a narrative pattern in which all speculation about the divine is abruptly displaced by the revelation of that which might actually

67

be a mark of the divine. Yet then again, it might not. This is Melville's aesthetics of doubt; and as every Melvillean knows, the issue becomes progressively more clouded and doubtful in Melville's later novels, *Pierre* and *The Confidence-Man*.

Or rather, shall we say that Melville works with a different yet equally legitimate conception from Emerson of what it means to acquaint men at first hand with the Deity? Emerson clearly had in mind the idea of the preacher becoming inspired before the eyes of his audience, a latter-day version of the kind of scenario Paul ascribes to the meetings of the early church: a summoning up of the Holy Spirit as sharable power. What Melville sought to acquaint men with was a different yet equally salient attribute of the divine: the Deity as mystery, the experience of Job, Chapter 23: "Oh that I knew where I might find him." At this point, revelation is on the point of becoming a null category, but – partly for that reason – a category that still holds a strong allure. As Rowland Sherrill remarks of both Carlyle and Melville, "the realization that silence is finally indefinable was consoled by their convictions that the world is plenteous with portents, however opaque, of the infinite."[28] Here indeed we have an important further key to the peculiar sort of repetition compulsion *Moby-Dick* evinces. Like Emerson, and in keeping with the post-Puritan sensibility in general, Melville was an avid reader of nature's spiritual "significances," but without the same confidence in the validity of those readings and in the doctrine of the mystical correspondence between spiritual and natural realms upon which Emerson could fall back. This uneasiness and anxiety did not, however, cause Melville's interest in reading nature to slacken, at least down through *Moby-Dick* and *Pierre;* on the contrary, at least in the short run, it acted as an energizing force, pushing Melvillean narrative in the direction of ever more elaborate, intense, ingenious, and repetitive sifting of nature's possible portentousness.

To the extent that *Moby-Dick* verges on revelation, what brand of revelation does it provide? T. Walter Herbert makes a strong case for the dominance of a particular ethnic strand in Melvillean thinking. "Melville," writes Herbert, "sets forth a Calvinistic analysis of Ahab's moral strife in order to form a drama in which Calvin's God appears morally odious on liberal principles, yet in

which liberal principles lose their validity as a description of religious truth,"[29] inasmuch as the wonder world through which
the *Pequod* sails seems to operate more according to the orthodox
vision of terror ("the invisible spheres were formed in fright"
[Chap. 42]) than in terms of the liberal vision of meliorism and
hope. This reading establishes *Moby-Dick* as a document in the
history of the clash in American and specifically northeastern post-
Puritanism between Reformation-Calvinist and Enlightenment-
Unitarian cross-currents, with Melville emerging as a sort of dis-
affected Calvinist. With this reading of Melville's religious ethnicity – a sophisticated version of the most prevalent view of the
subject – I fully concur. One further corroboration of it would be
the numerous parallels this reading suggests between Melvillean
sensibility and that of other contemporary post-Calvinist writers,
such as Emily Dickinson. Yet Melville's distinction from, say,
Dickinson, as a writer whose notion of revelation and myth ranges
far beyond the central post-Puritan lineage, ought also to be
stressed. Here Melville looks like a conservative counterpart of
Walt Whitman, both being concerned to make their images of
deity as comprehensively syncretistic as they can. Whitman is generally disposed to read those disparate traditions more affirma-
tively, as foreshadowing the new dispensation that he now proclaims, whereas Melville is more apt to play the graven images off
against each other in mockery. Both, however, strive to use their
ethnicity in "democratic" fashion, by converting an awareness of
the ethnocentrism of particular scenarios and imagings of revelation into scenarios and imagings that might serve as models,
positive or negative, for all the religions of the world. In this sense,
Moby-Dick, along with *Leaves of Grass,* stands as a great pioneering
work of comparative religion and as one of the most ambitious
products of the religious imagination that American literature is
likely to produce.

NOTES

1. On this point, see especially Nina Baym, "Melville's Quarrel with
   Fiction," *PMLA* 94 (1979):909–23.

2. John Guillory, *Poetic Authority: Spenser, Milton, and Literary History* (New York: Columbia University Press, 1983), p. 106.
3. Rowland A. Sherrill, *The Prophetic Melville* (Athens: University of Georgia Press, 1979), p. 100.
4. H. Bruce Franklin, *The Wake of the Gods: Melville's Mythology* (Stanford, Calif.: Stanford University Press, 1963), p. 61.
5. Robert M. Greenberg, "The Three-Day Chase: Multiplicity and Coherence in *Moby-Dick*," *ESQ* 29 (1983):91.
6. Franklin, *Wake of the Gods*, p. 66.
7. For further background on and analysis of religious themes in Melville's life and work, especially in *Moby-Dick*, the following works are very helpful: William Braswell, *Melville's Religious Thought* (Durham, N.C.: Duke University Press, 1943); Nathalia Wright, *Melville's Use of the Bible* (Durham, N.C.: Duke University Press, 1949); T. Walter Herbert, Jr., *Moby-Dick and Calvinism: A World Dismantled* (New Brunswick, N.J.: Rutgers University Press, 1977); and Bainard Cowan, *Exiled Waters: Moby-Dick and the Crisis of Allegory* (Baton Rouge: Louisiana State University Press, 1982), as well as the works by Sherrill and Franklin previously noted.
8. For further information, see especially Robert D. Richardson, Jr., *Myth and Literature in the American Renaissance* (Bloomington: Indiana University Press, 1978). See also the discussion of "Literary Scripturism" in Lawrence Buell, *New England Literary Culture: From Revolution Through Renaissance* (Cambridge: Cambridge University Press, 1986), chap. 7, the jumping-off point for the present essay.
9. See Merton M. Sealts, Jr., "Melville and Emerson's Rainbow," *ESQ* 26 (1980):53–78, for the most authoritative discussion of this and other aspects of Melville's contact with Emerson.
10. *The Collected Works of Ralph Waldo Emerson*, vol. 1, gen. ed. Joseph Slater (Cambridge, Mass.: Harvard University Press, 1971–), pp. 81, 80, 92–3.
11. Ibid., p. 92.
12. The distinction between scripture and hermeneutic is actually rather unclear. From a skeptic's viewpoint, this distinction is meaningless because sacred texts are nothing more than interpretation anyway. From a believer's standpoint, the distinction may still look flimsy because sacred texts (e.g., the New Testament) may be constructed around hermeneutical acts (e.g., that Jesus is the key to understanding the law and the prophets). Still, it seems valid to posit a distinction at least in principle between texts that claim to be divinely inspired – or are claimed to be – and texts that claim to be commentary

on the revelations of others, with a middle ground for projects like Emerson's in the *Address* that look for revelations within pre-established traditional or canonical restraints.

13. On this point, see especially Carl T. Jackson, *The Oriental Religions and American Thought: Nineteenth-Century Explorations* (Westport, Conn.: Greenwood, 1981).

14. Julie Ellison, *Emerson's Romantic Style* (Princeton, N.J.: Princeton University Press, 1984), p. 113.

15. Richardson, *Myth and Literature*, pp. 212–13.

16. For important examples of this approach, see especially Rodolphe Gasché, "The Scene of Writing: A Deferred Outset," *Glyph* 1 (1977):150–71; and John T. Irwin, *American Hieroglyphics: The Symbol of the Egyptian Hieroglyphics in the American Renaissance* (New Haven, Conn.: Yale University Press, 1980).

17. Franklin, *Wake of the Gods*, p. 64.

18. Another sort of stylization involved here is the tradition of the sublime. On Melville's use of this, see, for example, Barbara Glenn, "Melville and the Sublime in *Moby-Dick*," *American Literature* 48 (1976):164–82.

19. *Paradise Lost*, IV:268–75; *Home at Grasmere*, lines 788–94.

20. Ibid., lines 786ff: "Jehovah – with his thunder, and the choir/Of shouting Angels, . . . /I pass them, unalarmed."

21. Cowan, *Exiled Waters*, p. 162.

22. Zoellner, *The Salt-Sea Mastodon: A Reading of Moby-Dick* (Berkeley: University of California Press, 1973), p. 241. Zoellner carefully and very properly stops short of ascribing to Melville the explicit affirmation that Moby Dick is a supernatural and/or providentially directed being. Giles Gunn's commonsensical interpretation of the White Whale as symbol elaborates usefully: "Melville was much too deeply imbued with the spirit of Calvinism ever to confuse a manifestation of God's power, as Ahab does, with the very nature of God's essence, and he shared sufficient affinities with the Transcendentalists to doubt that God, if He exists, would ever become wholly and completely incarnate in a single form. If there is a God in the universe of this book, then Moby Dick is not that God himself but merely . . . the greatest among His creatures and one who, in his inscrutable but not entirely unknowable otherness, embodies as much of the principle of divinity as Nature expresses" (*The Interpretation of Otherness: Literature, Religion, and the American Imagination* [New York: Oxford University Press, 1979], p. 171). The reading of *Moby-Dick* of which this passage forms a part, and Gunn's earlier chapter on "Forms of Re-

ligious Meaning in Literature," shed additional light on matters treated in the present essay.

23. *Essays on Biblical Interpretation,* ed. Lewis S. Mudge (Philadelphia: Fortress, 1980), pp. 75, 81.

24. Ibid., p. 79.

25. In making this distinction, I do not mean to take a firm position on the issue of whether Ishmael actually ceases to become the narrator of portions of *Moby-Dick*. Although the final section and the earlier dramatic chapters provide support for such a claim, one could also argue that Melville has chosen to alternate between using Ishmael as conscious intermediary and using Ishmael as a conduit of vision.

26. Viewed in this light, Ishmael's method of narration begins to look like a counterpart of Ahab's "prophetic" rant: Both are mechanisms for coping productively with the trauma and memory of their former encounters with the White Whale.

27. Caserio, *Plot, Story, and the Novel: From Dickens and Poe to the Modern Period* (Princeton, N.J.: Princeton University Press, 1979), p. 149.

28. Sherrill, *Prophetic Melville,* p. 129.

29. See p. 128.

4

Call Me Ishmael, or How to Make Double-Talk Speak

CAROLYN PORTER

1

T HE voice that begins *Moby-Dick* by announcing "Call me Ish-mael" directs our attention immediately to a narrative perspective identified by its cultural dislocation, its displaced stance in a region somewhere beyond the borders of both the normal and the normative. By actively choosing the name of an outcast, Ishmael emphasizes his exiled stance. He proceeds to confirm if not his abnormality, at least his eccentricity, when he explains why he went to sea by adducing a series of reasons that culminate in the claim that going to sea is his way of avoiding suicide, his "substitute for pistol and ball." Yet he ends the opening paragraph by insisting that "if they but knew it, almost all men . . . cherish very nearly the same feelings toward the ocean with me" (Chap. 1). If Ishmael is first an exile whose very name invokes the boundary between outcast and society, by the end of the paragraph he has crossed that boundary to speak in the name of "all men." By shifting from eccentricity to normality, Ishmael establishes in embryo a pattern to be repeated and developed in the chapter as a whole, where boundaries are invoked in order to be crossed and finally blurred. First, and most notable, is the boundary between land and sea.

Ishmael begins by emphasizing the line dividing sea from land, focusing our attention on the "insular city of the Manhattoes . . . belted round with wharves as Indian isles by coral reefs" and surrounded by "commerce," so that we have before us an image of Manhattan as not only bounded but forcibly "belted" in. To the

73

water's edge have come "crowds of water-gazers" whom Ishmael describes as "leaning against the spiles" and "looking over the bulwarks," as if "striving to get a still better seaward peep." These "landsmen" seem to have poured down the "streets" that "take you waterward" in order to "get just as nigh the water as they possibly can without falling in."

The imagery of magnetism Ishmael uses to portray these water-gazing landsmen suggests that were they not "pent up in lath and plaster – tied to counters, nailed to benches, clinched to desks," the "magnetic" force exerted by the "compasses of all those ships" would compel them to emulate Ishmael in his decision to "sail about a little and see the watery part of the world." As Ishmael proceeds to multiply examples of the universal appeal of water, he not only calls forth the reader's assent to the claim that all men cherish a feeling for the ocean, but more importantly, he makes that feeling seem fundamental to human nature itself. In the interest of explaining his own desire to sail the seas as representative rather than exceptional, he has already begun to substitute sea for land as the locale of man's ontological condition, and thus to move us toward the position finally symbolized by Bulkington.

Appearing for the second and last time in "The Lee Shore," the chapter that marks the moment at which the *Pequod* leaves the shore, the figure of Bulkington not only provides Ishmael with an emblem of man's essential landlessness but also serves as a signal that we have already accompanied Ishmael across the boundary between land and sea. From this vantage point, it is no longer the sea that is dangerous. The land that once seemed our home, the scene of "safety, comfort, hearthstone, supper, warm blankets, friends," is now revealed as both "treacherous" and "slavish" when seen from across the *Pequod*'s prow (Chap. 23). But by now it is clear that to cross the boundary between land and sea amounts to more than a simple shift of perspective. The normal attributes of land and sea have been inverted, so that, once at sea, we are compelled to regard the land as inaccessible and our desire to return within its comforting limits as not only dangerous but suspect. For though "mortally intolerable," the conclusion to which Bulkington testifies is that "in landlessness alone resides the highest truth, shoreless, indefinite as God."

The rhetorical strategy used in Chapter 1 is designed, then, to loosen our attachment to the ground beneath our feet, so as to situate us eventually in Bulkington's position. As we will eventually learn, to embrace landlessness in these terms is to trade certainty for doubt and thus to find ourselves, like Ishmael, compelled not only to wander but to wonder. Crossing the border dividing sea from land ultimately threatens to blur all the categories of difference that order our apprehension of the world, bleaching it to a sinister and maddening whiteness. Ishmael's distinctive pattern of boundary crossing, then, operates to a purpose, a point that grows clearer as we observe his next rhetorical maneuver in Chapter 1.

Having invoked and then blurred the line between land and sea, Ishmael proceeds to subject the class divisions between passenger and mariner, officer and sailor, to similar treatment. Ostensibly, Ishmael wishes to specify the terms on which he sailed, and so to specify further his identity: "I do not mean to have it inferred," he begins, "that I ever go to sea as a passenger." Passengers are first distinguished from sailors by having a "purse," and a "purse is but a rag," Ishmael remarks, "unless you have something in it." In short, Ishmael's purse is empty. Yet this fact in itself eventually reveals a second reason for his shipping as a sailor rather than as a passenger: They pay sailors, "whereas they never pay passengers a single penny." Noting that "there is all the difference in the world between paying and being paid," Ishmael celebrates the joys of being paid in contrast to the pain of paying, "perhaps the most uncomfortable affliction that the two orchard thieves entailed upon us" (Chap. 1).

Since this discussion is divided into two parts and separated by Ishmael's related treatment of officers, the logical necessity at its heart is partially obscured; if someone is paying, someone else is being paid. To pay is to empty one's pockets and become the man in need of pay, whereas to *be* paid is to fill one's pockets and so be ready to pay again. Although there is a "difference . . . between paying and being paid," then, the line marking that difference begins to blur when the deed of paying and being paid actually takes place. When the roles of payer and payee are acted out, in other words, the actors can be seen constantly changing places with one another, a point of some consequence when, as here, these roles are designated by the class-defined terms of passenger and common sailor. In crossing the line rhetorically, Ishmael undermines its social force.

Initially embarrassed by poverty, Ishmael disclaims any desire to be a passenger; "passengers get sea-sick — grow quarrelsome — don't sleep of nights," he insists, as if his lack of money were a minor issue in his decision, an issue best treated in the abstract. But the very articulation of the abstract difference between paying and being paid serves rhetorically as the hinge by which Ishmael swings from the position of the man whose pockets have been emptied in the painful act of paying to that of the man happily anticipating being paid. He ends by imagining himself engaged in the "urbane activity" of receiving money, speaking now in the tones of the gentleman passenger when he ironically alludes to his Christian faith by noting how "marvellous" it is that we are so pleased to receive money when "we so earnestly believe money to be the root of all earthly ills."

Sandwiched within this discussion of passengers versus sailors, with its implicit subversion of class differences, is a treatment of sailors versus officers in which that subversion is made explicit. Here again, the pattern is repeated. The line dividing "a Commodore, or a Captain, or a Cook" from a "simple sailor" is drawn and then blurred. Indeed, Ishmael is already blurring it when he includes cooks in the same category with captains and commodores, since the cook we will soon meet on the *Pequod*, like many we might have met in the merchant service of the day, is a black. Abjuring as he does "all honorable respectable toils" carrying "glory and distinction," Ishmael confesses to a slight temptation when it comes to the "considerable glory" of being a cook. Yet it turns out that it is not the cook, but the cooked that attracts Ishmael, and so he displaces the honor due the "respectable toils" of the former onto the tastiness of the latter. "Once broiled, judiciously buttered, and judgmatically salted and peppered," he remarks, "there is no one who will speak more respectfully, not to say reverentially, of a broiled fowl than I will." Unless, he implies, it be the "old Egyptians" whose "idolatrous dotings . . . upon broiled ibis" resulted in "their huge bake-houses the pyramids."

The reverential language of honor attached to captain and commodore is first undermined by its transference to cooks and then exploded by its application to broiled fowl as the object of idolatry.

It remains for Ishmael to face squarely the socially degraded status of the common sailor. After a bravado gesture worthy of Whitman, presenting himself as the sailor "right before the mast, plumb down into the forecastle, aloft there to the royal masthead," Ishmael admits that no matter how far and wide he may move, he moves at the dictates of others. "They rather order me about some," he acknowledges, but when he adds that they "make me jump from spar to spar, like a grasshopper in a May meadow," his simile evokes an image of springtime freedom already undermining the force of the point it illustrates. Ishmael then marks the line between sailor and officer in terms that give it both personal and social resonance when he notes that such treatment "touches one's sense of honor, particularly if you come of an old established family in the land, the Van Rensselaers, or Randolphs, or Hardicanutes." In itself, the implication that Ishmael comes from such a family begins to destabilize the very social division he is acknowledging, for if a common sailor can be the son of a gentleman, class lines are already blurred. Further, the juxtaposition of the Van Rensselaers and the Randolphs with the Hardicanutes, whose demise has long since been accomplished, obviously serves to relativize and so undercut the force of the "old established family" as a social category.

But finally, in order to blur the line between officer and sailor effectively, Ishmael must address the core issue of authority, of who gives and who takes, orders. Noting that his "transition . . . from a schoolmaster to a sailor" has been a "keen one," Ishmael appeals to the authority of the New Testament and the viewpoint of the "archangel Gabriel," in whose eyes all men are spiritual equals. From this perspective, "who aint a slave?" Ishmael asks, and goes on to insist that "however much they may thump and punch" him, the "universal thump is passed round" in a circuit that includes "everybody." As in the case of paying and being paid, the roles of thumping and being thumped are passed around, and so the distinction loses its significance, if not from a "physical" at least from a "metaphysical point of view."

Although the class line between captain and sailor has been seriously questioned and its force partially suspended, it is important to notice that it has by no means disappeared. Such boundary lines, whether between land and sea or between gentleman and sailor, are crucial to Ishmael's discourse. They must be there if they are to be crossed and blurred, whether by appeals to the New Testament's teaching on spiritual equality and the evils of money, or by the burlesque on flatulence with which Ishmael concludes his commentary on the commodore, who "gets his atmosphere at second hand from the sailors on the forecastle."

Ishmael rounds out the chapter by invoking and then blurring the line to which he will return in "The Mat-Maker," that between fate and free will. From the start, Ishmael has accounted for his decision to ship as a common sailor in terms that presuppose that it *was* a decision. Indeed, the entire chapter up to this point derives much of its ironic force from the disparity between Ishmael's tone of reasoned judgment and the personal exigencies clearly behind his alleged choices. But faced with the need to explain his choice of a whaler as his berth, Ishmael falls back on Fate and the "grand programme of Providence." He now insists that Fate dictated his choice, all the while cajoling him into the delusion that it was a "choice" made by an "unbiased freewill and discriminating judgment." But at the same time, he turns Fate itself into a joke. He takes the "programme of Providence" literally, excerpting it when he lists "whaling voyage by one Ishmael" as an event in small print squeezed in between "Grand Contested Election for the Presidency of the United States" and "Bloody Battle in Afghanistan." He humbly admits his inability to explain why "those stage managers, the Fates," gave him "this shabby part of a whaling voyage," whereas others were accorded roles in "high tragedies" or "genteel comedies" or "farces," leaving to our judgment which genre fits events such as the "grand contested election for the presidency."

In closing the chapter, Ishmael returns to the point where he began, the magnetic attraction of water, now objectifying it in the "overwhelming idea of the great whale himself." Swayed by the attractive force of the "mysterious monster" and the "wild and distant seas where he rolled his island bulk," Ishmael returns across the boundary between normality and eccentricity as he admits that "with other men, perhaps, such things would not have been inducements." But he can now afford to acknowledge that his "itch for things remote" may be idiosyncratic because he has now established a narrative voice that commands some authority over its own territory — a no-man's-land, a marginal space between the known and the unknown. By transgressing boundaries, by subverting the force of fixed oppositions, Ishmael has established a voice that can now move back and forth across them with head-spinning speed: "Not ignoring what is good, I am quick to perceive a horror, and could still be social with it — would they let me." The lines dividing good from evil, familiar from alien, individual freedom from coercive force, are crossed in swift succession, in a passage that itself carries us from the rebellious freedom of sailing "forbidden seas" and landing on "barbarous coasts" to the image of the world as a prison where "it is well to be on friendly terms with all the inmates" (Chap. 1).

2

A narrator who persistently blurs the very distinctions to which he appeals in introducing himself and his story speaks from a peculiar position, one likely to make extraordinary demands upon us as readers, forced as we are into a dizzying effort to keep up with a voice we justifiably suspect is bent upon carrying us away — away from our moorings among familiar assumptions and out to a sea where all assumptions are in doubt. But our troubles are as nothing compared to Melville's. To understand how Ishmael's voice is empowered, his unique perspective authorized, is to appreciate both the problems Melville faced and the skill with which he solved them.

Where, to begin with, do you ground the perspective of a narrator who resembles those "judicious, unincumbered travellers in Europe" who "cross the frontiers into Eternity with nothing but a carpet-bag, — that is to say, the Ego?" So, in a famous letter to Hawthorne, Melville characterized those men who had the courage to say "No! in thunder" to the age's smug beliefs.[1] To praise such a man, however, is one thing; to give him a voice and a place to stand is another.

We have already begun to see how Melville met this problem in *Moby-Dick*. As Ishmael crosses and blurs the boundary dividing sea and land, his voice takes up residence *at* the boundary, occupying the marginal space between the familiar and the unknown that he creates and expands by traversing it, over and over again. In other words, Melville turns the boundary itself into the locus of Ishmael's narrative voice.

Yet such a voice remains necessarily unstable, since it is always undermining the very boundaries from which it speaks. Such instability, indeed, becomes part and parcel of Ishmael's identity as narrator. He is, for example, notorious for reporting soliloquies he cannot pretend to have witnessed, and indeed, for disappearing entirely on occasion. Further, he shows only the most sporadic respect for the ordinary conventions of narrative, such as plot or character development. Yet there is a rhetorical method in his narrative madness, one we can appreciate more fully by broadening our focus from the opening chapter to the opening movement of *Moby-Dick*, Chapters 1 through 23, which take us from Ishmael's self-introduction to the moment marked by "The Lee Shore," the moment when the *Pequod* plunges "like fate into the lone Atlantic" (Chap. 23).

These twenty-three chapters depict Ishmael's own "waterward" course to Nantucket, and his preparations for setting sail – preparations both "physical" and "metaphysical." These chapters also serve to prepare *us* as readers for setting sail by establishing both the commercial (physical) and the religious (metaphysical) implications of the voyage to come. Yet it is Ishmael's meeting with Queequeg and their developing friendship that provides the novel's opening movement with its narrative center. Not only are nine of the twenty-three chapters centrally concerned with Queequeg, but once he appears in Chapter 3, we never lose sight of him completely, even in Father Mapple's chapel.

Queequeg's prominence is the more striking in view of the fact that he will play a far smaller role in the story to come than we are led to expect here. So marked is the disparity between his introduction in the novel's opening section and his diminished role in the rest of the tale that it has served as evidence for the theory of the "two *Moby-Dicks*."[2] Yet whatever its compositional history, the misleading prominence of Queequeg in these chapters as they stand in the finished text can best be accounted for by understanding his role as essentially played out by the time he and Ishmael set sail – the role of initiating Ishmael into the tribe of the whalemen, those "renegades and castaways" of all colors and cultures who make up an "Anacharsis Clootz deputation" representing a global citizenry of marginal men, or what Ishmael calls "Isolatoes" (Chaps. 26–27). Queequeg's presence continues to be felt, to be sure, but largely as a result of the bond formed in these chapters, a bond so deep that Queequeg becomes virtually a double, a shadow self for Ishmael. That bond must be secured at the outset if Ishmael is to assume full membership in the company of whalemen. In short, as he becomes "social" with the particular "horror" that is Queequeg, Ishmael's unstable narrative identity is provided with a social dimension.

In becoming Queequeg's "bosom friend," Ishmael is subjected to a cultural identity crisis from which he emerges with the social identity required to support the narrative perspective we have begun to observe in action. Ishmael's encounter with Queequeg – his initial fear, his weakening defenses, both "melting" into a profound love and admiration for the cannibal – is less an extended episode in a story than a passage through a "liminal" state in which the boundaries between civilized and savage, Christian and cannibal, are simultaneously crossed and blurred.[3] But Ishmael's ritual initiation deviates markedly from the pattern set by earlier accounts of travel among savages, in which the encounter with alien people serves to reconfirm the boundaries of the civilized.

For example, Richard Henry Dana, Jr.'s, *Two Years Before the Mast*, which set many of the conventions for the travel adventure of Melville's day, presents a young voyager who rounds Cape Horn and lands on the coast of California, where he encounters a host of alien creatures, with one of whom he even becomes good friends.[4] Yet throughout his narrative, Dana remains an observer whose ultimate crisis, significantly, centers on getting home. Initiated into the hard life of a sailor and exposed to a host of culturally alien customs and people, Dana undergoes a rite of initiation that leads back to Boston and to his reconfirmed sense of himself as a gentleman. He crosses boundaries, to be sure, but only to return with a renewed sense of his original civilized self.

Nor is the pattern that informs Dana's narrative limited to the literary realm. As T. Walter Herbert has shown, the encounters with the South Sea Islanders recorded in the travel accounts of Charles Stewart and David Porter display the same reconfirmation of the civilized self.[5] We will have occasion to return to these models shortly, but for now they can serve to point up the singularity of Ishmael's case. For Ishmael hardly emerges from his encounter with Queequeg as a reconfirmed member of civilized society. On the contrary, he has become the "bosom friend" of a cannibal with whom he has formed a lasting bond of love, ritually celebrated in a pagan rite (Chap. 10). Having crossed the boundary between civilized and savage, he does not return. Yet neither is he transformed into a savage cannibal himself. Rather, he finds himself on the border between the two realms, translated by his bond with Queequeg into a man alienated from civilized society, and yet an alien to the savage world from which Queequeg has come. He thus resembles no one more than Queequeg himself.

It is worth recalling that Queequeg has left a royal family behind on his native island. Like Ishmael, he has responded to an "itch for things remote" by leaving home to sail about the world (Chap. 1). And like Ishmael, he now finds himself suspended between two worlds. In "Biographical," we are told that "Queequeg's wild desire to visit Christendom" proved so strong that he forced a Sag Harbor captain to let him stay aboard his ship, and was forthwith "put down among the sailors and made a whaleman." So, like Ishmael, he has been precipitously demoted from the upper to the lower classes, and, like Ishmael, he has "disdained no seeming ignominy" as a common sailor, despite his noble origins (Chap. 12). Further, Queequeg's biography mirrors Ishmael's, for Queequeg has crossed the boundary between the savage and the civilized from the other side, yet with similarly alienating results.

Queequeg's motives for impressing himself into the ship's company ironically mirror the missionaries' motives for spreading the gospel in the South Seas: "he was actuated by a profound desire to learn among the Christians, the arts whereby to make his people still happier than they were; and more than that, still better than they were." Discovering that Christians are both "miserable and wicked," he has decided to "die a Pagan" but has remained an exile, living "among these Christians" and trying "to talk their gibberish." No only alienated but corrupted, Queequeg believes himself now "unfitted for ascending the pure and undefiled throne of thirty pagan Kings," contaminated as he is by his exposure to "Christianity, or rather Christians" (Chap. 12).

Melville's ironic inversion here of the story Americans were telling themselves about the savages, whose culture they were in fact contaminating and destroying in the name of Christianity, presupposes the rhetorical strategy at work throughout his treatment of Queequeg. He situates Ishmael and Queequeg together by a double process; as the alien grows familiar, the familiar grows alien, so that Queequeg is no longer a startling, multicolored savage but a man with a biography, and one that resembles Ishmael's in key respects.

This process has already begun in Chapter 6, "The Street," where, after spending his first night with Queequeg, Ishmael saunters out "for a stroll" in New Bedford. His initial "astonishment" at seeing "Queequeg circulating among the polite society of a civilized town" fades in the light of day and the now apparent fact that this "civilized" seaport is populated not only by sailors but by "savages outright." To see "actual cannibals stand chatting at street corners" renders the cannibals familiar and the street corners strange. To see among the "Feegeeans" and "Tongatabooans" the "green Vermonters" makes the latter "more comical" and equally alien. "New Bedford is a queer place" indeed, where the rich live in "patrician-like houses" fenced in by "iron emblematical harpoons." Not only do Queequeg's peculiarities turn out to be normal, but the normal becomes strange, until finally the line between civilized and barbaric is impossible for Ishmael to discern. It is the barbaric whalemen, after all, who are responsible for civilizing New Bedford itself; "Had it not been for us whalemen, that tract of land would this day perhaps have been in as howling condition as the coast of Labrador," Ishmael concludes (Chap. 6).

Melville has foreshortened the matter of the alien encounter, then, and encapsulated it in the novel's opening section. He puts his narrator through an initiation into pagan life from which he emerges not, as convention demands, at the end of a voyage but at the outset of one, and not with a reconfirmed identity but with a radically fluid one. The outcast who introduced himself as Ishmael has, by forming a bond with a cannibal, joined that company of whalemen and other "queerest looking nondescripts" he finds populating an allegedly civilized New Bedford as well as the decks of the *Pequod*.

Yet the social identity thus accorded Ishmael's narrative voice only complicates Melville's task; for an alliance with such sailors and savages hardly renders Ishmael respectable or trustworthy as a narrator. A man who speaks from what Melville's contemporaries regarded as the margins of civilization, from what Americans today still marginalize when they refer to it as the Third World, is ill-placed, to put it mildly, for authorizing his voice. Ordinarily, the travel writers of Melville's day commanded authority by speaking from a position securely fixed within the society for which they wrote. Thus, Dana narrates his adventure from the perspective it served to resecure — that of the young Boston gentleman. The narrative itself steadily maintains its distance upon the alien worlds of both ship and shore that Dana observes. Similarly, in David Porter's account of the Marquesas, the natives are objects — of observation, coercion, and finally slaughter. In Charles Stewart's account, they are objects ripe for conversion.[6] In *Moby-Dick*, savages and sailors retain their otherness, but they are not regarded as objects at a distance. Ishmael, as he tells us, "was one of that crew" (Chap. 41).

In short, insofar as the voice of Ishmael has acquired a habitation and a name, it is neither local nor familiar. Further, what kind of discourse is available to a man who speaks from the boundaries? To occupy Ishmael's position entails what his voice everywhere reveals — a deeply subversive relation to all forms of discourse. The discourse of savages and sailors remains alien and unauthorized, whereas those authorized by his own culture are necessarily subjected to an alienation effect that distances and renders them suspect. In short, Ishmael's voice may have been grounded in a social identity, but the question remains, how is his discourse to find authority?

It is this question of how to authorize the discourse of a socially marginalized and culturally alienated narrator that takes us to the heart of Ishmael's rhetoric in *Moby-Dick*. But to understand Melville's solution to this problem, at once a literary and a personal one, we need to return to the point at which it first arose for him, at the outset of his career as a writer. When he published *Typee* in February, 1846, Melville was already crossing and blurring a boundary, although he did not yet know it. He was not, however, allowed to remain in ignorance for long.

3

On April 17, 1846, *The Morning Courier & New York Enquirer* reviewed *Typee*, damning it as a "fiction." Conceding that the author may have "spent some time in the Marquesas Islands," the reviewer nonetheless insisted:

> We have not the slightest confidence in any of the details, while many of the incidents narrated are utterly incredible. . . . This would be a matter to be excused, if the book were not put forth as a simple record of actual experience. It professes to give nothing but what the author actually saw and heard. It must therefore be judged, not as a romance or a poem, but as a book of travels – as a statement of facts; – and in this light it has, in our judgment, no merit whatsoever.[7]

In this reviewer's view, Melville had violated the boundary between fact and fiction. His charge, moreover, was echoed on both sides of the Atlantic. Some skeptics, indeed, questioned whether Melville had even *been* to the Marquesas, and the more sardonic of them went further, asking whether "Herman Melville" was a real person.[8]

In crossing and blurring the line between fact and fiction, the young author committed a sin whose seriousness in Melville's day Michael Bell has recently demonstrated.[9] Modern scholarship, moreover, has found him guilty. As Leon Howard sums up the case, *Typee* "well deserved to come under suspicion."[10] Among other things, Melville altered the time span from the four weeks he had actually spent on the island to the four months recorded in the narrative. He portrayed a lake on an island that has none. He borrowed from previous accounts by Stewart, Porter, Ellis and Langsdorff, although disavowing such debts.[11]

Given such departures from fact, what are we to make of Melville's claims that *Typee* is "based upon facts . . . which have come immediately under the writer's cognizance"? (p. xiv) By and large, critics have interpreted Melville's responses to his reviewer's skepticism as covering up the bad faith of an incipient romancer. Thus, after a close scrutiny of the Preface Melville composed after his English publisher, John Murray, had voiced his skepticism, Leon Howard concludes, "Caught by a publisher's unanticipated demand that his 'yarn' be certified as the 'truth', he could only ask with jesting Pilate 'What is truth?' and evade, as best he could, the answer" (p. 293).

Given the demonstrated fictional elements in *Typee,* and given the subsequent record of Melville's capacity for ironic duplicity toward his readers, it is hardly surprising that we have come to view Melville's first book as the product of an imagination already caught in the act of disguising itself. Since *Typee* is not entirely factual, in our sense of the term, we have come to interpret his responses to the charges at the time that it was a fiction as the evasions of an author caught out in lies he at least half knew he had told. Yet the evidence adduced for Melville's conscious duplicity in the matter is far from compelling, and points just as persuasively, if not more so, to a different claim: Melville kept insisting that he had told the truth because he really believed he had.

For one thing, his letters at the time reveal a man alternately befuddled and outraged by people who insist on not believing him. The more his word is questioned, the more ardently he seeks to defend it. Indeed, when we look at his correspondence, it is hard to believe that this twenty-seven-year-old novice author was yet capable of the duplicities charged against him by modern scholars. Consider, for example, his response to the *New York Enquirer*'s hostile review. Melville composed a piece to be placed anonymously in the same newspaper and sent it to a friend who had agreed to serve as conduit. The piece itself has not survived, but the letter accompanying it reveals a man whose deep discomfort with *this* duplicitous act is readily apparent:

> Herewith you have the article we spoke of. I have endeavoured to make it appear as if written by one who read the book and believed it – & moreover – had been as much pleased with it as most people who read it profess to be. Perhaps, it may not be exactly the right sort of thing. The fact is, it was rather an awkward undertaking any way – for I have not sought to present my own view of the matter (which you may be sure is straightforward enough) but have only presented such considerations as would be apt to suggest themselves to a reader who was acquainted with & felt friendly toward the author.[12]

Aware that his own name cannot be used, since it is after all his own word that is in doubt, Melville has written a friendly review of his own book, and even "modelled" it "upon hints suggested by some reviews" already published.[13] His closing remarks make it clear that he has been driven to this stratagem by his fear that the "obnoxious review," now widely reprinted, will "do mischief unless answered," impairing "the success of the book here as a genuine narrative."[14] As a travel writer, Melville may already have behaved deviantly, but he is not yet comfortable with being devious.

In any case, Melville never deviated from his insistence that *Typee* was essentially accurate, except implicitly when he cut from the revised edition the passage in which he disclaimed any knowledge of Porter's or Stewart's accounts of their Marquesan visits. Whether he had read these accounts when he actually wrote this early passage is unclear. That he *had* read them at least by the time he completed the manuscript has been demonstrated.[15] That he chose to eliminate his claims to the contrary *may* reveal that he had originally lied, but it surely indicates a desire to correct any such misrepresentation.

Nor does Melville's rhetoric in the Preface to *Typee* necessarily support Howard's interpretation of duplicity. The Preface is clearly designed to win the reader's confidence, and was no doubt composed, as Howard notes, after Melville "had been put on the defensive by John Murray's queries and demands." Howard reads the Preface as a series of evasions designed to excuse the author from the duties of a "meticulous historian," and finds even Melville's closing insistence upon his "anxious desire to speak the unvarnished truth" telling for its failure actually to state "that he *had* spoken the unvarnished truth" (p. 293).

Yet when we read the Preface not in order to find traces of guilty evasion, but simply as the testimony of an author whose word has been doubted, what first strikes us is his sustained attention to his readers' expectations as these have been determined by the conventions of the travel narrative as he understands it, and his overriding desire to explain his deviations from such conventions in terms that will inspire the reader's confidence.

For instance, he notes that unlike other "writers of travels among barbarous communities," he "refrains in most cases" from trying to account for the "origins and purposes" of their peculiar "customs," and asks to be excused for this "culpable omission" in the light of the "very peculiar circumstances in which he was placed" (p. xiii). Again, he acknowledges the prominent attention normally accorded "dates" in "many published narratives," but explains that since he "lost all knowledge of the days of the week," he could not follow this convention (p. xiv). And again, he explains his partial orthographic deviation from "several works descriptive of the islands in the Pacific" on the grounds that these works have often failed to convey "many of the most beautiful combinations of vocal sounds . . . by an over-attention to the ordinary rules of spelling" (p. xiv).

In each case, Melville explains his deviations from convention on the grounds dictated by his actual experience. Howard treats such rhetoric as a ploy, yet it need not imply the conscious duplicity of motive Howard infers when he says, for example, that when Melville explained the lack of dates, he was trying "to protect himself against the one charge which fortunately was not raised but to which he knew he was most vulnerable – that of falsifying the time period" (p. 293). It is just as likely that Melville's strategy here is more directly concerned with accounting for his break with the convention – one used by Dana, for example – of ordering a travel narrative by reference to dates, than with consciously covering up deliberate falsehood. He was certainly aware, of course, that he had extended the length of his adventure, but he was also very likely telling the truth when he said that he had lost track of time while on the island. The point is that we need not read any conscious duplicity into Melville's defensive strategy here in order to account for a rhetorical maneuver more simply explained by the hypothesis that he was struggling to make his story credible by connecting it to the tradition of travel writing to which he saw himself contributing at this point in his career. By apologizing for his deviations from this tradition, he simultaneously drew himself more visibly into the company of others whose testimony had been credited and authorized with the public.

The Preface does deserve a skeptical reading, but its tensions derive less from a conflict between the truth of Melville's experience and the account he had delivered in the pages to follow than from a conflict between that account and the assumptions informing the genre upon which his readers' expectations were based. For if Melville's aim here is to buttress the authority of his testimony by bringing it more closely into relation with the conventions of travel writing, he is also palpably aware that beneath the conventions he has innocently violated lie a set of values and beliefs he has not so innocently called into question. In other words, the source of the rhetorical strain in the Preface lies in the cross purposes to which Melville is driven when forced to ground his credibility as author in a tradition whose authority he has also questioned in the text to follow.

Accordingly, while paying homage to that tradition by begging forgiveness for his deviation from its conventions, he cannot avoid registering his awareness of what such deviations actually signal – a positive difference from, and in some cases a repudiation of, the accounts whose veracity he himself is questioning. For example, the polite disclaimer of any explanations concerning native customs acquires its irony from the fuller explanation provided in the text proper for this "culpable omission": "There is a vast deal of humbuggery in some of the accounts we have from scientific men concerning the religious institutions of Polynesia." (p. 170) It is after all those who have *not* omitted such explanations who are "culpable." On this reading, the Preface reveals a Melville less concerned to cover his tracks than to authorize his perspective, by trying to ground it in a tradition whose conventions and dominant values he has actually violated.

In effect, Leon Howard is right, but for the wrong reasons. Melville's readers did have good reason to be suspicious, not because of the extent to which he had embellished his tale, but rather because of the threat his narrative posed to their culturally inscribed defenses. Nor was this threat merely a matter of *Typee*'s outspoken attacks on the civilizing missionaries. Rather, it was Melville's marked tendency to "dismantle" the civilized self, as T. Walter Herbert has put it, which provoked such outrage.[16] As narrator, Tommo not only deliberately depicts, but unwittingly reveals, a dismantled self, one whose partial absorption into an alien culture has destabilized his perspective far more seriously than Melville apparently realized at the time of writing. If, as Herbert has argued, Melville adopted in *Typee* the narrative perspective of the "gentleman-beachcomber," he remained largely innocent of the radical instability of such a contradictory synthesis.[17] He spoke as a gentleman, but his views were too often those of the beachcomber, a marginal man, half proletarianized by his shipboard life as a sailor, half estranged by his four years of exposure to foreign peoples with dark skins.

Thus his genuine astonishment when faced with such "numbskulls," as he called them, who "heroically avow their determination not to be 'gulled'."[18] "How indescribably vexatious," he wrote to Murray in response to a request for "documentary evidences," when "one really feels in his very bones that he has been there, to have a parcel of blockheads question it."[19] Melville could not comprehend the charges brought by his skeptical reviewers because they were questioning his authority in terms that served to obscure the root source of their stated doubts. They accused him of lying; he insisted he had told the truth. But the two parties to this quarrel were already speaking different languages.

As Michael Bell has made clear, in mid-nineteenth-century America the distinction between fiction and nonfiction was far more central than that between the novel and the romance. Indeed, according to Bell, Hawthorne's careful effort to carve out the romance as his province, and to define its limits and operative assumptions, was itself a defensive strategy designed to undermine the suspiciousness with which fiction was regarded by those of his contemporaries who regarded it as contaminated by imagination and riddled with deceit. The line between fiction and nonfiction was charged defensively against the multiple dangers seen in the increasingly popular fictional forms invading the literary market-place.[20]

In a larger sense, the opposition between fact and fiction operated variously to mark off the true from the false, the good from the bad, the healthy from the diseased, the real from the illusory, the honest from the deceitful. In effect, the distinction between fiction and nonfiction became charged by the very threats it had arisen to defuse, and thus was likely to be invoked most forcefully when threatened most directly. This *Typee* accomplished. The popular travel narrative achieved its credibility as factual not, finally, by any scrupulous attention to dates or orthography but by the distance it preserved, and even reinforced, between civilization and savagery, familiar and alien, safe and dangerous. By collapsing that distance, Melville's narrative voice called into question the opposition it ordinarily served to maintain. His narrative therefore became, for many readers, literally incredible. Whatever the embellishments and inventions Melville had used to make his narrative entertaining, these were not the source of the skepticism voiced by his reviewers. These readers, after all, did not have before them the evidence adduced by modern scholarship. Their incredulity arose in response to a narrative voice that was itself destabilized by the experience it sought to report, and that therefore destabilized their own most basic assumptions about the world.

Thus, because he had blurred the line between the civilized and the savage, Melville was accused of violating that between fiction and fact. Nor could he counter such charges. His only recourse was to underscore his book's generic identity, and his own class identity, by means of the rhetorical alliance he attempted in the Preface to the revised edition of *Typee*. Just as in *Typee* proper, he could only call the line between civilized and savage into question from a supercivilized vantage point that depends for its authority on the very category of the civilized that he was questioning,[21] so in the

Preface he can only authorize his word by relating it to that of the very authorities whose word he is questioning. It is this same double bind, however, in which narrative authority must be derived from the discourse of those whose authority he is questioning, that Melville ultimately unravels and exploits in order to authorize Ishmael's voice in *Moby-Dick*.

Before returning to Ishmael's voice, it is worth noting that the distinction between fiction and nonfiction in Melville's early work, an issue to which scholars have devoted considerable attention, needs to be resituated in relation to the struggle for narrative authority that began with *Typee*. Among other things, this approach would allow us to relate Melville's tendency to mix fictional and nonfictional genres to the well-known story of his hostility to his audience.[22] For example, when Melville shifted from the nonfictional travel narrative to the romance in *Mardi*, he cryptically prefaced his book by announcing his decision "to see whether the fiction might not, possibly, be received for a verity; in some degree the reverse of [his] previous experience."[23] The experiment failed, to be sure, but we have not fully appreciated all that was at stake for Melville in it.

We have generally seen *Mardi* as a turning point in Melville's career because it reveals him moving away from fact toward fiction, a view that quite logically leads to the conclusions reached by Nina Baym when she argues that Melville's adoption of fictional genres proved incompatible with his consistent aim of truth telling.[24] Truth, displaced from the factual to the fictional, from the physical to the metaphysical realm, turned out to be impossible to tell, according to Baym, and Melville's career as a fictionist is thus marked by a serial rupture of genre after genre, as each proves resistant to the truth teller's efforts. On this view, Melville's unwavering devotion to the "great Art of Telling the Truth" was only frustrated by his choice of fiction as a medium.[25]

No doubt this is accurate enough, and yet it obscures an issue just as basic to Melville's needs and aims here. If we take seriously the implicit challenge he hurled at his audience in *Mardi*'s Preface − "You want a romance? I'll give you a romance!" − it becomes clear that Melville made the shift to fiction at least in part in an effort to find a discourse in which his voice might be authorized.

Encompassing and motivating the search Baym has described Melville pursuing, for a fictional genre in which to tell the truth, is a fundamental and longer-lived need to find an authorized discourse. In a sense, Melville was seeking the authority he felt he had lost at the very moment he had claimed it, the authority of his own word. Underlying the shift from nonfiction to fiction, and woven throughout his quarrel with a hostile and indifferent audience, is a search for some authority to replace that which turned up missing in *Typee*.

If we followed Melville's career to its end from this vantage point, we would see more clearly why he finally abandoned fiction. For eventually, fictional discourse by itself would prove as unreliable a source of authority as nonfictional discourse had, operating as it did in accord with codes of consistency and verisimilitude that became, to Melville, manifestly false. He bid farewell to fiction with *The Confidence-Man*, whose implicit motto could have echoed that with which he turned away from nonfiction in *Mardi*: "You want to be gulled? I'll gull you!" His subsequent career as a poet, a choice itself partly informed by the same need to authorize his voice, only continues a long and tortured story in which Melville found that the truth lacked authority, and that authority – the authorized discourses of his era – lacked truth.

Yet at the center of that career is *Moby-Dick*, a book whose extravagant violations of generic boundaries have always rendered it virtually unclassifiable, whereas the imaginative genius of its language continues to outstrip our expectations at each reading. For once, Melville found a narrative voice fully adequate to the demands he placed on it. This is not to say that only with *Moby-Dick* did he succeed as an artist – far from it. Nor is it to suggest that *Moby-Dick* was met with widespread praise. It was not. Nor is this lack of responsiveness surprising, for in Ishmael, Melville created a narrator who speaks with the full authority of the culture whose authority he is out to subvert.

4

Ishmael, as we have seen, blurs boundaries for a purpose. He aims to undermine our most basic and fixed assumptions and beliefs, to destabilize our culturally inscribed patterns of perception, to de-center our rooted perspective as landsmen. He ought to be a threat. Yet he has usually been regarded by modern readers as genial, tolerant, open-minded – in short, as a comic and sane counter-weight to the mad Ahab. Although Ishmael's narrative rela-tionship to Ahab, as we shall see, contributes to this effect, the major source of Ishmael's miraculous talent for radically de-stabilizing our perspective without provoking our hostility lies elsewhere – in his double-voiced discourse.[26] It is such discourse, in fact, that enables him to cross and blur boundaries with im-punity, for it allows him to voice the other, the alien, while osten-sibly speaking the language of the culturally legitimate.

We can see such double-voiced discourse at work most clearly in those chapters like "The Affidavit," where Ishmael speaks a readily identifiable language. Here it is the lawyer who under-takes, with characteristic circumlocution, to "take away any in-credulity which a profound ignorance of the entire subject may induce in some minds, as to the natural verity of the main points of this affair." Disavowing any hope of proceeding "methodically," Ishmael nonetheless tries to provide a legal brief, consisting in "separate citations of items" from which "the conclusion aimed at will naturally follow of itself." The first group of such items is divided into two categories, personal and general knowledge, and the "conclusion aimed at" is that specific, identifiable whales can be and have been encountered twice by the same whalemen, thus making plausible Ahab's calculated pursuit of the particular whale that dismasted him. The second group demonstrates that the "Sperm Whale is in some cases sufficiently powerful, knowing, and judiciously malicious, as with direct aforethought to stave in, utterly destroy, and sink a large ship." The chapter is punctuated with firstly's and secondly's, and replete with lengthy quotations from texts whose "testimony," Ishmael assures us, is "entirely independent of my own" (Chap. 45).

Yet Ishmael's legalistic format breaks down almost immediately, as if the eager witness had become befuddled by the need to organize his "items" in so artificial a form. He claims to have "personally known three instances" in which a whale has been harpooned, escaped, and "been again struck by the same hand."

94

But instead of enumerating each instance in orderly fashion, he confuses them to the point of absurdity. He seems particularly obsessed, for example, with the "three year instance," in part no doubt because it echoes, and seems to underscore, his opening claim that he knows of three instances of a harpooned whale being reharpooned by the same man. The number three is repeated nine times in the course of one paragraph: five times in reference to the number of years between first and last encounters, three times in reference to his instances, and once as a guess regarding how many times the whale in the three year instance "circumnavigated the globe." Meanwhile, no doubt in an effort to stretch the interval between first and second sightings, he twice qualifies the three year instance, which "may have been something more than that," at least he is "pretty sure it was more than that." This, despite the story he tells about the man who reencountered the whale in the three year instance, a man who happened "in the interval" to join a trading ship to Africa, go ashore, and travel inland with a "discovery party . . . for a period of nearly two years" (Chap. 45). It is not that one couldn't resolve these apparent contradictions by reconstructing Ishmael's argument. The man in question could have spent two years in Africa, returned to sea, and some time later, at least a year and probably "something more than that," met up with his whale. The point is that as Ishmael recounts such "instances," they are garbled by the very numbers designed to organize and verify them.

Nor is the purpose of verification served by the little flight of fancy used to depict the three year instance man's African adventure, in which he was "endangered by serpents, savages, tigers, poisonous miasmas, with all the other common perils incident to wandering in the heart of unknown regions." Ishmael clearly wants to emphasize the improbability of the man's second encounter with his whale; he moves deep into Africa while the whale is "brushing with its flanks all the coasts of Africa," and yet both are unwittingly set on a course that will lead them back to each other. But the more Ishmael tries to make his primary point – that such encounters are not as unlikely as they may seem – the more confused his argument becomes. Digression gives way to the simple and repeated insistence, "I say, I, myself, have known three

instances . . ." The reductio ad absurdem arrives with his claim
that in the three year instance he was "on the boat, both times,"
and recognized the whale by the "huge mole" under its eye
(Chap. 45).

Since the three year instance is taken from an actual account,
which Melville could have simply quoted, as he in fact does with
other accounts later in the same chapter, Ishmael's peculiar handling of his evidence obviously results from a deliberate strategy.[27]
He is, of course, parodying the legal discourse he struggles so
arduously to deploy, but the effect of this form of parody is complex. As it keeps collapsing, Ishmael's visible effort to marshall his
argument behind "separate citations of items" ends by discrediting
not his own word but the legal discourse in which he tries to
speak. In other words, if the passage were fully ironic, the parody
would undermine Ishmael's credibility altogether, sweeping his
claims into the heap of refuse that is piled up by his "instances"
and "items." Yet because his struggle with the language of the
"affidavit" is so palpable, it is the language, and not his testimony
itself, that is discredited. At the same time that it is being parodied
and discredited, however, this legal language is already beginning
to authorize the very voice that fails to speak it successfully. Ishmael's veracity is actually being supported by his audible inability
to fit what he knows to be true into the conventions inscribed in
the testimonial discourse. Rather than regarding his evidence as
doubtful, we begin to feel that the truth does not sound like
evidence.

There are, in effect, two voices speaking here. One speaks in the
cadences of legal testimony, and the other can be heard struggling
against its limits. But the second voice can be heard only because it
clashes so discordantly with the first. Indeed, that is why the legal
discourse is voiced in the first place: to make audible the voice that
cannot speak it fluently. The purpose, then, is not only to parody
legal discourse but to circumscribe and reify it, so that its boundaries come into view, set in relief as an artificial limit against the
expanse of alien knowledge Ishmael has no direct means of com-
municating. Consequently, Ishmael's voice is authorized ironically, by its capacity to expose the limits of the authorized dis-

course in which he is compelled to speak. In the act of parodying legal discourse, he usurps its authority.

Here Ishmael's authentic voice sounds against the legal discourse because he so audibly fails to master its conventions, but this is only one means by which double-voiced discourse is set into operation in *Moby-Dick*. Ishmael is by no means always so incompetent. On the contrary, he often reveals so profound a mastery of the discourse he is voicing that he can apply it readily to novel areas of knowledge or experience. But the effect is similar; the limits of the parodied discourse are exposed at the same time that its authority is appropriated. For example, in the next section of "The Affidavit," Ishmael adopts the pose of a learned authority on the "Sperm Whale Fishery."

"It is well known in the Sperm Whale Fishery," he begins, "however ignorant the world ashore may be of it," that "a particular whale" becomes "popularly cognisable," a fact to which "several memorable historical instances" attest. Here, the Sperm Whale Fishery designates the whaler's ocean world as if it were a specific delineated realm, a nation to itself with its own history, which Ishmael is engaged in describing to us from behind a lectern. Translated into this historian's pedagogical discourse, tall tales become cultural history in which particular whales acquire their fame from a "terrible prestige of perilousness" to which "the fatal experiences of the fishery" give rise (Chap. 45).

The information Ishmael proceeds to deliver about "famous whales" actually comes from whaler's lore, the kinds of stories that other writers kept at arm's length in their accounts. Thomas Beale, for example – a major source for Melville throughout *Moby-Dick* and a specific source for this passage – regards such "strange" stories as that of "Timor Jack" as "probably much exaggerated."[28] Ishmael himself has already acknowledged the "fabulous rumors" abounding in the Sperm Whale Fishery. In Chapter 41, "Moby Dick," he has made it clear that he knows a tall tale when he hears one, but this does not prevent such tales from circulating at sea to profound effect, as when "some whalemen" are found to believe that Moby Dick is "ubiquitous" and "immortal" (Chap. 41). Thus, "Timor Jack" becomes "Timor Tom" in his account, in which the very fact that the whale has a name serves to corroborate his claim that "famous whales enjoy great individual celebrity" in the Sperm Whale Fishery (Chap. 45). Speaking as one of the "students of Cetacean History," to whom such names are "as well known as Marius or Sylla to the classic scholar," Ishmael becomes the historian of an alien world, but one after all no more alien than the Roman. Indeed, he has himself been so deeply absorbed by the culture of the Sperm Whale Fishery that he speaks finally as its epic poet in a series of apostrophes: "Was it not so, O Timor Tom . . . O New England Jack! . . . O Morquan! . . . O Don Miguel!" This momentary seizure is itself foregrounded as epic discourse when Ishmael abruptly concludes it by returning to "plain prose." In such a passage, Ishmael immerses us in the alien culture of the Sperm Whale Fishery by means of a learned discourse appropriated from the shore world. As the discourse itself is parodied, it serves to authorize not only a knowledge to which it is alien, but the very voice that is engaged in the parody.

In "The Affidavit," the ironically self-authorizing effects of Ishmael's double-voiced discourse are unusually clear. As the parody grows more extravagant, Ishmael himself grows more persuasive. He ends the chapter by extending the scope of his "historical instances" back to the sixth century and Procopius's account of a sea monster, which Ishmael construes, by means of a manifestly preposterous reasoning process, to "have been a sperm whale." The alien worlds of the Sperm Whale Fishery and the Romans are forced to coalesce here, in a parody of the speculative historian intent upon bending his evidence to suit his argument. "A fact . . . set down in substantial history," Ishmael insists, "cannot easily be gainsaid"; never mind that he has admitted the "substantial history" in question to be faulty "in some one or two particulars" and the "fact" in question to be far too vaguely reported to count. The "precise species" of Procopius's sea monster is not mentioned, but Ishmael clears up this detail by resorting to a marvel of circular reasoning. He has been arguing for several pages that the sperm whale is capable of destroying ships. Now he decides that the sea monster must have been a whale, "as he destroyed ships" (Chap. 45).

In this extravaganza, Ishmael repeatedly makes explicit reference to "the best authorities" whose discourse he is simultaneously parodying. Where before he spoke as the fully initiated epic poet of the Sperm Whale Fishery, here he seems to embrace just as thoroughly the landsman's logic (a tactic he will employ to similar effect in "Jonah Historically Regarded"). Yet as before, the parodied discourse serves primarily as a sounding board for Ishmael's authentic voice, as if he were a ventriloquist smiling at the nonsense his own dummy is made to speak. By voicing the discourses he is constrained to speak through, Ishmael submits them to an alienation effect, while all the time appropriating their authority. As a result, this chapter can actually serve the purpose for which it is named. As an affidavit, it can disarm skepticism. At least it did for one reviewer at the time. After reading Chapter 45, he said, "all improbability of incongruity disappears, and Moby Dick becomes a living fact, simply doubtful at first, because he was so new an idea."[29] Although hardly representative, this reviewer's response testifies to the potential power of Ishmael's double-voiced discourse as a strategy for usurping authority.

The same double effect can be seen in Ishmael's parodic voicing of scientific and philosophical discourses, where the authority inscribed in the landsman's culturally bound and legitimized discourses is both undermined and exploited, enabling Ishmael to cross and blur boundaries in the name of the boundary keepers themselves.

In Chapter 32, "Cetology," for example, he opens with his characteristic humility, avowing his inability to perform the task before him — "the classification of the constituents of chaos." Yet in this case, such helplessness immediately allies him with "the best and latest authorities" who, like Beale, themselves attest to the "utter confusion" that "exists among the historians of this animal." "Cetology" is a chapter famous for its parody of erudite naturalists, and nowhere is Ishmael more explicit in his appeal to existing authorities, actually listing their names, from "the Authors of the Bible" on through Coffin, Olmstead, and Cheever. The cetological information Ishmael provides here is largely plundered from such sources, as is the metaphor of sovereignty, taken from Beale, which Ishmael weaves through his discussion, though to an effect far beyond any predictable from Beale.[30] Thus, "the Greenland whale is an usurper upon the throne of the seas" whom Ishmael proclaims "deposed" by the "great Sperm Whale" who "now reigneth." Again, despite Linnaeus's declaration, "I hereby separate the whales from the fish," Ishmael insists that "down to the year 1850, sharks and shad, alewives and herring, against Linnaeus's express edict," swam "the same seas with the Leviathan." (Insofar as Linnaeus unwittingly echoes God in Genesis, Ishmael parodies the same source.) But if whales and fish refuse to abide by the edict of "A.D. 1776" and separate themselves, Ishmael himself usurps Linnaeus's authority when he denies pig-fish and saw-fish "their credentials as whales" and dismisses them from "the Kingdom of Cetology." In short, Ishmael mixes the discourse of the naturalist with that of political sovereignty, just as he organizes his cetological information by reference to the sizes of books, in accord with the fact that "though of real knowledge there be little, yet of books there are plenty" (Chap. 32).

Here, then, Ishmael in effect uses one discourse to satirize another, so that the authorities whose voices he is parodying undermine each other. Meanwhile, Ishmael's voice absorbs the authority it is all the while draining from these discourses, which are left beached, as it were, like those "uncertain whales" whose names are "mere sounds, full of Leviathanism, but signifying nothing" (Chap. 32).

As this allusion to *Macbeth* indicates, Ishmael's voice is by now a virtual sponge, capable of soaking up an infinite number of voices and squeezing out their discourse into a pool as large as the ocean he sails. The scholarship devoted to tracing Melville's borrowings and allusions in *Moby-Dick* is itself comparably infinite.[31] Nor have critics failed to note that, as Joseph Flibbert puts it, Melville "parodies his source at the same time that he plunders it for information."[32] What I wish to add is that he plunders his sources for their authority as well, a rhetorical feat that relies upon Ishmael's double-voiced discourse.

Understood as the locus of such discourse, Ishmael represents a solution to the problem of self-authorization that Melville had first confronted when met with the skeptical responses to *Typee*. For if Ishmael's voice operates, as I have argued it does, to absorb the authority of the very discourses he parodies, then he serves as a rhetorical device skillfully designed to exploit the double bind by which Melville was trapped in the Preface to *Typee*. But Ishmael is more than a rhetorical solution to Melville's long-standing problem. He is also the narrator of *Moby-Dick*, and his role in the novel requires further scrutiny.

5

Ishmael's double-voiced discourse, although not limited to his digressive chapters, explains one of their major purposes, for in these long-winded digressions, Ishmael's voice not only absorbs authority but disperses it. As a narrator who has begun by assuming a stance on the boundaries, allied there with socially marginal outcasts, Ishmael ends by speaking in the name of a global community of men, "an Anacharsis Clootz deputation" representing the human race at large (Chap. 27). The digressions on whaling, from "Cetology" to "The Whiteness of the Whale," from "The Advocate" to "The Affidavit" and beyond, are crucial to this process.

Having undergone his ritual initiation at Queequeg's hands into the world of the Sperm Whale Fishery, Ishmael, as we have seen, acquires the social identity of the whaleman. He immediately begins establishing his professional credentials in "The Advocate," a chapter that parodies oratorical debate in its defense of the honor and dignity of "the business of whaling." By means of the same double-voiced discourse we have seen him deploy in "The Affidavit" and "Cetology," Ishmael appropriates for the whale ship the honor accorded "Martial Commanders" and the "heroes of Exploring Expeditions," whose exploits have opened access to distant lands and thus enlarged the scope of "the enlightened world" (Chap. 24). As usual, Ishmael is undermining the values inscribed in the discourse he uses, exposing its contradictions right and left. "If American and European men-of-war now peacefully ride in once savage harbors," he declares, it was the "whale-ship which originally showed the way," as if war ships brought peace, as if the proud Americans were not literally "men-of-war," as if "savage harbors" had not been peaceful themselves prior to such civilizing invasions. Yet at the same time that he exposes the rhetoric of imperialism, Ishmael is himself expanding the provenance of his voice, enlarging its scope by according the Sperm Whale Fishery the status it deserves. What begins as self-parody, when Ishmael remarks how "ridiculous" it would be for a harpooner to add the initials "S.W.F." to his "visiting card," ends with the avowal that "a whale-ship was my Yale College and my Harvard" (Chap. 24). As he mimics the rhetoric of honor and respectability, Ishmael empowers his voice as that of a cosmopolitan and professional.

By the same token, as he voices the discourses of philosophers, scientists, and politicians, Ishmael absorbs their authority, displacing it to the society of whalemen, whose esoteric knowledge and marginal status thereby become normal, even normative. In short, such digressions provide Ishmael with the sea room he needs to move from social outcast to social spokesman. As a member of the Anacharsis Clootz convention that the *Pequod's* crew symbolizes, Ishmael gives voice to an alien sea world. But he does so by speaking through and against the familiar discourse of the shore, and in the process he displaces and disperses the latter's authority, delivering it over to the democracy of the "meanest mariners, and renegades and castaways" he represents (Chap. 26).

Yet as embodied in the *Pequod's* crew, Ishmael's discursive democracy reveals remarkably little capacity to resist virtually total submission to Ahab's authority. It is not only his institutionalized authority as captain, but a primitive tribal authority to which the crew subject themselves in the pagan ritual described in Chapter 36, "The Quarter-Deck." When we recall that Ishmael was "one of that crew" and filled with a "wild, mystical, sympathetical feeling," welding his "oath" to "theirs," his rhetorical behavior as narrator is cast in a different light (Chap. 41). If, by subverting and appropriating the authority inscribed in the discourses he voices, Ishmael is enabled to blur the boundaries between the familiar and the alien with impunity, his narrative position on the boundaries also serves to construct − for both himself and his reader − a defense against the threat represented by Ahab.

Ahab's authority is beyond the reach of Ishmael's parodic voice. A mark of Ahab's discursive impunity is his tendency to speak in monologues. Ahab talks primarily to himself, addressing others only in the line of duty to his overarching obsession, as in "The

Quarter-Deck," where he ignites the crew with the fire of his maniacal zeal. Although he must use language to achieve his ends, Ahab's authority over the crew finally depends less on his verbal discourse than on the discourse of ritual, dramatic action he manipulates so skillfully. Accordingly, Ahab comes to us as a man incapable of dialogue, for conversation as a social medium requires at least the equality of a shared discourse, even if not of a shared social status, and Ahab shares neither. Even when he appears to converse, Ahab places his interlocutor at such a distance that, like the carpenter, he is justified in asking, "What's he speaking about, and who's he speaking to?" (Chap. 108). Only with Fedallah does Ahab seem to enjoy the communion of genuine dialogue, but finally as the quest for Moby Dick reaches its climax, the two "never . . . speak," so "yoked together" are they by "the unseen tyrant driving them" (Chap. 130).

Except with the Parsee, then, when Ahab speaks he is performing either before his company, as on the Quarter-Deck, or for himself, as in the following chapter, "Sunset." Yet his performance is by no means fraudulent. When he conducts the ritual designed to merge the crew's will with his own, he himself participates fully, with no ironic distance. And when he talks to himself, he is similarly fully present in his own speech. Yet it is *not* his speech, but that of Lear and Hamlet, among others, that flows from his mouth. Because Ahab hears no speech but his own, he cannot recognize that it is not his own that he speaks. He is a man possessed, wholly in the grip of the inspired language he speaks, just as he is totally consumed by the demon within that drives him along "iron rails" to his "fixed purpose" (Chap. 37). Just as Ahab acknowledges no boundaries to his will, he exhibits no sense of discursive boundaries. Whether he is talking with others or speaking from Shakespeare's stage, Ahab is always addressing the blank, mute universe he so woefully inhabits, trying to get a voice out of silence but doomed to hear nothing but his own voice, since he is deaf to the voices of others.

Yet this very discursive isolation both reflects and fosters Ahab's autonomous authority. Acknowledging no other authority than himself, Ahab seizes all authority for himself. In relation to his crew, he does so by an appeal to atavistic instincts; in relation to the reader, he does so by a discourse purified by amnesia of any "mortal inter-indebtedness" to others (Chap. 108). In this sense, Ahab represents a wish fulfillment on Melville's part, for his discursive amnesia enables Melville to pose the ultimate questions in a voice charged with epic energy but owning allegiance to no authority save its own.

Ahab's authority, then, lies beyond the range of Ishmael's double-voiced discourse for the same reason it exerts such a powerful attraction, for Ahab's authority seems to be self-generated. Like the godlike Prometheus, "who made men, they say," Ahab taunts Starbuck with the question, "Who's over me?" (Chaps. 108, 36). Yet although he claims that he would "strike the sun if it insulted" him, Ahab is revealed as in thrall himself to the sun's element (Chap. 36). If "right worship is defiance," what Ahab worships "defyingly" as the "clear spirit of clear fire" is the devil, in whose name he baptizes his harpoon, just as Melville was to baptize his book (Chap. 119).[33] Owning his allegiance to the "speechless, placeless power" of fire, Ahab allies himself with the fires of hell; "for what's made in fire must properly belong to fire," he says, "so hell's probable" (Chaps. 119, 108). An authority wholly generated out of the self, in short, is an authority doomed to serve the forces of evil.

Ahab's power, then, is irresistible because demonic, sealed by a pact with the devil – Fedallah, Ahab's dark shadow self – and manifested in his capacity to subordinate the crew's will by "magnetically" charging them with "the same fiery emotion accumulated within the Leyden jar of his own magnetic life" (Chap. 36). Even Starbuck cannot finally resist the primitive power upon which Ahab depends to divert the *Pequod* from its appointed economic ends. Given that Ishmael has testified to the sea's magnetic attraction for him, and that he has already undergone a ritual transformation in becoming Queequeg's friend, it is hardly surprising that his "shouts had gone up with the rest" (Chap. 41). As "one of that crew," Ishmael is irresistibly drawn by the force of Ahab's will, by the self-generated authority he exercises over the ship and aims to impose on nature itself.

Yet in telling his tale, Ishmael develops a rhetorical defense against the threat that Ahab's fatal quest unveils. If his narrative stance on the boundaries enables Ishmael to undermine the landsman's authority, it also enables him to resist the threat of absolute boundary violation that is at the heart of Ahab's madness.

Ahab's obsessive revenge is, after all, itself a response to the violation of his boundaries — as free man, as autonomous human, as whole body. Ahab's boundaries, both physical and metaphysical, have been violated so decisively that he has been driven mad. As his empathy with Pip's madness reveals, Ahab has survived an experience in which the lines dividing man and nature, self and world, have dissolved. His monomaniacal quest, then, is fueled by the need to resecure the boundaries that Moby Dick has violated. As Michael Rogin has argued, Ahab's obsession is itself a defense "against chaos, against the panic of rage without a target."[34] Ahab's madness derives from the dissolution of the most personal as well as the most universal of boundaries, for not only has the integrity of his body been violated, but the integrity of his mind and his soul as well. The white scar that some believe runs from Ahab's "crown to sole" brands him as a man riven in two, clinging fast to a monomaniacal purpose that alone holds him together. His vengeful pursuit of the White Whale is fueled by a need as desperate as it is doomed, the need to reinstate the boundaries that the whale's dismembering attack has dissolved. But as the case of Pip serves to indicate, once such boundaries have been dissolved, they cannot be reconstituted. For the vision of chaos and the experience of absolute vulnerability to which such a crisis leads render all boundaries suspect, artificial, and finally sinister. All "visible objects" become for Ahab "pasteboard masks," and for Ishmael, "though . . . this visible world seems formed in love, the invisible spheres were formed in fright" (Chaps. 36, 42).

Wonder ye then, as Ishmael might say, at the value of clinging to the boundaries? To cross and blur boundaries is one thing; to violate them absolutely, another. Just as Ishmael requires the discourses of others to make his own voice heard, he depends upon the authority invested in those discourses as a virtually infinite resource on which to draw, not only for his own authority as narrator, but also as a defense against the threat inscribed in Ahab's autonomous authority — the threat of total annihilation. As Robert Zaller has argued, rebellion is for the Melvillean hero a dialogue with power in which assassination must be avoided because it would break the circuit.[35] By the same token, Ishmael never kills the authority vested in the discourses he parodies; rather, it is as if he borrows the authority of one, then another source. His stance on the boundary, then, not only enables him to blur it but to defend it against the total dissolution that would render him, like Pip, a mad mimic rather than a sane one.

This built-in resistance to the magnetic attraction of Ahab's demonic authority underlies Ishmael's ability to destabilize without threatening us as readers, to make us "social" with the "horror" to which he opens our eyes. Ishmael both subverts authority and clings to it, just as he advises us to cling to the Mast-Head. For to blur all boundaries is to lose one's footing, as has Ahab, who would "like to feel something in this slippery world that can hold" (Chap. 108).

In his desire for a self-generated authority, Ahab served Melville as an expressed wish fulfillment, but his mad captain also testifies to Melville's fear of boundary dissolution, the same fear that provided *Typee* with its dramatic suspense: Will I be eaten by these friendly natives? In Ishmael, however, he constructed a narrative perspective that could express both wish and fear with impunity. By speaking from the boundaries in a voice authorized by the very discourses it subverts, Ishmael is empowered to defend against the very threat of boundary dissolution to which this stance makes him vulnerable. In the Epilogue, as in the story it concludes, Ishmael floats "on the margin," and though "drawn towards the closing vortex," he is miraculously saved. Just as Queequeg's friendship accorded him a socially designated place to stand on the boundary between civilized and savage, Queequeg's coffin provides him with a "life-buoy" on which he floats along "a soft and dirge-like main," unharmed by "sharks" and "sea-hawks," until the *Rachel* appears to find "another orphan." As reported, Ishmael's survival is almost as implausible as his narrative behavior is outrageous, but both reflect the "cunning spring" and "buoyancy" of his double-voiced discourse (Epilogue).

NOTES

1. "To Nathaniel Hawthorne," April 16, 1851, *Moby-Dick*, ed. Harrison Hayford and Hershel Parker (New York: Norton, 1967), p. 555.
2. George R. Stewart, "The Two *Moby-Dicks*," *American Literature* 25 (January 1954): 417–48.
3. On liminality, see Victor W. Turner, *The Ritual Process: Structure and Anti-Structure* (Chicago: Aldine, 1969).
4. Richard Henry Dana, Jr., *Two Years Before the Mast* (New York: Penguin, 1981), pp. 207ff.
5. T. Walter Herbert, *Marquesan Encounters* (Cambridge, Mass: Harvard University Press, 1980).
6. For a brief but useful discussion of Dana's narrative perspective, see Thomas Philbrick's Introduction to *Two Years Before the Mast*, op. cit., pp. 7–29. For an extended analysis of Porter and Stewart, see Herbert, *Marquesan Encounters*, pp. 51–148.
7. Jay Leyda, *The Melville Log*, 2 vols. (New York: Harcourt, Brace, 1951), vol. I, pp. 211–12.
8. "A doubt has existed on the part of some reviewers, whether it is the genuine production of the reputed author." Ibid., vol. I, p. 228. For an overview of the skeptical reception accorded *Typee* and then *Omoo*, which was contaminated by association, see ibid., vol. I, pp. 204–49. An example of the sardonic reviewers: "The train of suspicion once lighted, the flame runs rapidly along. . . . And Herman Melville sounds to us vastly like the harmonious and carefully selected appellation of an imaginary hero of romance. . . . Of the existence of Uncle Gansevoort, of Gansevoort, Saratoga County, we are wholly incredulous." Ibid., vol. I, p. 249.
9. Michael Davitt Bell, *The Development of American Romance* (Chicago: University of Chicago Press, 1980).
10. "Historical Note" in Herman Melville, *Typee: A Peep at Polynesian Life*, ed. Harrison Hayford, Hershel Parker, and G. Thomas Tanselle (Evanston, Ill: Northwestern/Newberry, 1968), p. 291.
11. See Charles R. Anderson, *Melville in the South Seas* (New York: Columbia University Press, 1939).
12. Leyda, *Log*, vol. I, p. 214.
13. Ibid.
14. Ibid., pp. 214, 215.
15. Anderson, *Melville*, pp. 117–78.
16. Herbert, *Marquesan Encounters*, p. 178.
17. Ibid., p. 153.

18. Leyda, *Log*, vol. I, p. 214.
19. Ibid., p. 236.
20. Bell, *American Romance*, pp. 25–36.
21. Herbert, *Marquesan Encounters*, pp. 152–5.
22. For the best introduction to Melville's relationship to his audience, see Ann Douglas, *The Feminization of American Culture* (New York: Alfred A. Knopf, 1977), pp. 349–95.
23. Herman Melville, *Mardi, and A Voyage Thither*, ed. Harrison Hayford, Hershel Parker, and G. Thomas Tanselle (Evanston, Ill: Northwestern/Newberry, 1970), p. xvii.
24. Nina Baym, "Melville's Quarrel with Fiction," *PMLA* 94 (October 1979): 909–23.
25. "Hawthorne and His Mosses," in Hayford and Parker, ed., *Moby-Dick*, p. 542.
26. The term "double-voiced discourse" is taken from Mikhail Bakhtin, on whose theory of language and the novel the following discussion draws heavily. See "Discourse in the Novel" in Bakhtin, *The Dialogic Imagination*, trans. Caryl Emerson and Michael Holquist (Austin: University of Texas Press, 1981), pp. 259–422.
27. The account is Henry T. Cheever's, and the relevant passage is provided in "Explanatory Notes," *Moby-Dick*, ed. Luther S. Mansfield and Howard P. Vincent (New York: Hendricks House, 1952), p. 720.
28. Ibid., p. 720.
29. William T. Porter, "Spirit of the Times," in *The Recognition of Herman Melville*, ed. Hershel Parker (Ann Arbor: University of Michigan Press, 1967), p. 47.
30. Thomas Beale's use of the metaphor of sovereignty is apparent in the passage cited in "Explanatory Notes," Mansfield and Vincent, ed., *Moby-Dick*, p. 674.
31. A start on this infinitude may be made with F. O. Matthiessen, *American Renaissance* (New York: Oxford University Press, 1941), and the "Explanatory Notes" in Mansfield and Vincent, ed., op. cit.
32. *Melville and the Art of Burlesque*, in Robert Brainard Pearsall, ed., *Melville Studies in American Culture*, Vol. 3 (Amsterdam: Rodopi N.V., 1974), p. 65.
33. "To Nathaniel Hawthorne," June 29, 1851, in Hayford and Parker, ed., *Moby-Dick*, p. 562.
34. *Subversive Genealogy: The Politics and Art of Herman Melville* (New York: Alfred A. Knopf, 1983), p. 115.
35. "Melville and the Myth of Revolution," *Studies in Romanticism* 15 (Fall 1976): 607–22.

Calvinist Earthquake: *Moby-Dick* and Religious Tradition

T. WALTER HERBERT, JR.

OLIVER Wendell Holmes's "The Deacon's Masterpiece, or The Wonderful 'One-Hoss Shay'" likens Calvinist orthodoxy to a carriage constructed of parts so perfectly in keeping with one another that the system has no "weakest point."[1] This paragon of self-sustaining logic is completed on the first of November in 1755, the day of the Lisbon earthquake. It runs exactly 100 years without a single breakdown, and in the midst of the parson's morning drive on the first of November in 1855, at the very moment the earthquake had struck, it uniformly and instantaneously disintegrates. The parson is left sitting on a mound of fine particles, rather like cornmeal, which is all that remains of the shay.

This lighthearted satire reduces the inexorable logic of Calvinist doctrine to the relations of felloe, thill, prop-iron, and thoroughbrace in the shay, technical terms with an antique ring parodying such momentous tenets as "irresistible grace," "indefinite atonement," and "moral inability." Holmes was quite right in judging that such items of belief, and even the great central issues of providence and original sin, were losing their power over the religious imagination of Americans in the mid-nineteenth century.

The spiritual convulsions attending the death of Calvinism are evoked here very delicately; it is Holmes's intention to dismiss the grim old apparatus, not to grapple with its angularities. Yet his allusion to the Lisbon earthquake reminds his readers of the issues over which a century of religious turmoil had taken place. The

I wish to express my gratitude for the generous assistance provided by Warwick Wadlington, Winston Davis, and Richard Brodhead.

sudden collapse of the shay is featured as an aftershock of the disturbance occurring when it was put together.

The earthquake at Lisbon reduced two-thirds of the city to rubble, killed some 20,000 people, and would as a matter of course have called forth a religious response as survivors sought to rebuild their lives. The religious concern aroused by incomprehensible suffering reaches well beyond Calvinist culture and may be native to religious life in all societies.[2] But on this occasion there took place, in effect, a second earthquake: an intense religious conflict whose irreconcilable oppositions arose from a deep unstable fault in the Calvinist tradition of theology and religious practice as it developed in Northern Europe and America, a fault that had already generated a substantial history of disturbance by the mid-eighteenth century. The tradition itself disintegrated in Melville's time, as these fundamental incongruities came to a head.

Calvin's doctrine of providence was the crux of the matter: He held that "the world is so governed by God that nothing happens in it except by His *secret counsel and decree.*"[3] This doctrine means that the truth about the nature of the universe and the unfolding of human experience is what God has ordained. Calvinists also believed that the central institutions of society, as well as the minutiae of daily life, should be regulated by the divine truth thus made known. At first, it seems a patent contradiction: God's will controls everything that happens in the world, and believers devote their lives to making what happens in the world conform to his will. Yet more than one revolutionary creed has demonstrated that men and women may display astonishing self-discipline and self-sacrifice in seeking to bring about what they devoutly believe to be inevitable.

The historical impact of the Calvinist temperament is well known to have been immense; it includes, at a minimum, the congregational and presbyterian forms of ecclesiastical organization, the Puritan revolution, and the establishment of a Puritan "city on a hill" in the New World. Debates continue regarding its influence upon other historical developments, notable for their breadth and variety: the rise of capitalism and the decline of magic, the political organization of the United States and the creation of politics in the modern sense, the structure of common law and the routinization of time.[4] In the early nineteenth century it was common sense in America to believe that all great historical achievements arise from a religious motive, and succeed or fail depending on whether they correspond to God's truth.

Yet from the moment of its articulation Calvin's doctrine of providence was attacked, first by Roman Catholics and then by a series of dissenters from Michael Servetus to Jacob Arminius, who asserted that the doctrine denied human freedom and made God the "author of sin." Put bluntly, the problem was that the God whose justice was the very definition of moral truth seemed himself to act unjustly, since he ordained the sins that men commit. This dilemma, touching the central axioms of the faith, prompted John Milton's grand resolve in *Paradise Lost,* to

> . . . assert eternal Providence
> And justify the ways of God to men.

Milton's solution depends for its credibility upon the notion of collective guilt: that the human race is fallen because of its participation in the sin of Adam, a sin that Adam (according to Milton, not Calvin) was at liberty not to commit. Yet as the seventeenth century gave way to the eighteenth, a conception of individual right increasingly took hold, portraying human beings not as wholly lost in sin, but as rational and moral beings innately capable of choosing between good and evil, and of attaining a substantial degree of virtue. Deists like John Toland aggressively set forth a vision of religious truth in keeping with this doctrine, and there grew up among dissenters and Wesleyan Methodists an increasingly liberal Protestant Christianity in which God's control of what happens in the world was qualified, as the rational and moral powers of man were accorded greater scope. By mid-century the work of Alexander Pope and Voltaire had made famous this vision of human dignity, strengthened as it was by the achievements of the human mind in revealing the laws governing the physical universe. Deists and liberal Christians looked out upon a created order in which natural law and moral law alike testify to a benign creator and a morally competent humankind.

Then the earthquake struck, the indiscriminate slaughter vindicating Calvinist belief and throwing liberals into confusion.[5] To

111

Calvinists, the earthquake was only a conspicuous instance of God's truth as it is apparent everywhere in the created order of things, the misery that God inflicts upon human beings in his righteous anger at the depravity into which the whole race has fallen. Calvinists were entirely prepared to agree that the victims of the earthquake deserved to die, since they believed that the survivors also deserved to die, God having chosen to spare them not on account of their relative moral worth, but simply because it was his sovereign will to do so. If God were not justly enraged by human sin, Calvinists asked, why would he ordain a natural order in which men are *"formed to be the living prey of Bears and Tygers . . . given up to be crushed and churned between the Jaws of Panthers and Leopards, Sharks and Crocodiles?"*[6]

Holmes's reference to Lisbon indicates his awareness that the Calvinist system gained strength from its capacity to account for such calamities, in which the moral inexperience of children, or the virtue that adults may attain, make no difference in the ruin and suffering that befall them. But this explanatory power was gained at the expense of a principle that deists and liberal Christians were increasingly unable to relinquish: the belief that human beings are able to cultivate an inherent moral dignity that is God given and that God is morally bound to respect. In America, moreover, the success of the Revolution imparted a numinous aura to the contention that men "are endowed by their creator with certain inalienable rights," and as the nineteenth century unfolded, this article of democratic faith deepened its hold.

This dilemma lies at the heart of *Moby-Dick,* where Ishmael and Captain Ahab come to terms with a whale whose career of wanton destruction suggests a God run amok. "All his successive meetings with various ships contrastingly concurred," Ishmael observes, "to show the demoniac indifference with which the white whale tore his hunters, whether sinning or sinned against" (Chap. 130).[7] Melville recognized that the remorseless logic of orthodox Calvinism was not only consistent with itself; it was also consistent with realities of human experience that cannot be explained by the theory that God respects liberal conceptions of human dignity. Melville further recognized that orthodoxy and liberalism represent alternative elaborations of the shared premise at the center of

Calvinist religion: the belief that the course of worldly affairs embodies the will of a God who rightfully demands worship and obedience.

Melville challenges this Calvinist axiom by invoking the dilemmas it created on both sides of the tradition. He was intimately familiar with the theological formulations by which liberal and orthodox believers sought to resolve those dilemmas for themselves, and with the language in which they accused each other of being hopelessly enmeshed in confusion. *Moby-Dick* reverberates throughout with allusions to specific doctrinal tenets and the controversies regarding them, and with invocations of scriptural passages as they were characteristically glossed by liberal and orthodox partisans. Melville's famous comment on Hawthorne, in which he speaks of a "Calvinistic sense of Innate Depravity and Original Sin," has misled certain students into assuming that Calvinistic issues figure in *Moby-Dick* only in a generalized way, as an offset to Melville's democratic ebullience and as an accessory of his major interests, which are frequently considered to be aesthetic rather than religious.

Yet *Moby-Dick* is a work like the Book of Job, or Augustine's *Confessions*, or Coventry Cathedral, or Benjamin Britten's *War Requiem*, in which art and the sacred are fused. Also like these works, *Moby-Dick* conveys an apprehension of religious reality that is innately turbulent, in notable contrast to the sacralization of rational order and moral order that is native to Calvinist religion, and indeed to the tradition of religious art that predominates in the West between the time of Augustine and the twentieth century. Instead of envisioning a logically integrated system of ideas that can account for (and regulate) everything that happens, Melville portrays religious reality as a shaking of the foundations. It is not the decorous city with its routines and elaborate structures where Melville finds godhead, but the ground on which the city stands, which reveals its strange hidden life when it moves.

Melville does not attack traditional ideas about God with the object of replacing them with better ideas; his mission is prophetic, that of calling us to a deeper life. He is a forerunner of religious writers in our own time, like Dietrich Bonhoeffer and Elie Wiesel, whose keynote is the maintenance of discourse concerning ultimate realities in the face of horrors so extreme as to confound religious meditation altogether, to threaten it with extinction. Yet unlike Bonhoeffer and Wiesel, Melville does not speak for a community of religious teaching and observance. He invokes traditional theological materials in such a way as to produce a characteristic dissonance, in which conflicting perspectives are pressed upon the reader simultaneously. By this means, Melville continuously establishes and disestablishes the reader's relation to his narrative; at every point, we find ourselves struggling to find a framework in which to place what is being said.

Melville thus draws us into a religious struggle. The traditional perspectives at work are biblical and theological, pointing toward the ultimate boundaries of experience; and Melville places the unresolvable conflict of these perspectives at the book's own outermost horizon, embracing within that horizon a discourse concerning final questions, the meaning or unmeaning of life and death. Engaging in that discourse, as it goes on in passage after passage, calls up a religious consciousness; and as we attempt to place Melville's local meanings within the context of the work as a whole, we are carried to the frontier at which the churning of interpretive frameworks goes on, Melville's dismantling and reframing of the world.

The relation of Ishmael and Ahab is a primary structural element of the narrative that aids in generating this ontological instability. The two never exchange a word in the long course of the voyage, yet they are linked as figures of a spiritual crisis. Religious controversialists in Melville's time became aware that, as the controversies grew more elaborate and intractable, they appeared increasingly trivial to the public at large. The "truth" over which the contestants were fighting progressively lost authority, so that by 1853 Holmes could treat the whole matter as a joke. Liberal and orthodox writers blamed each other for this encompassing dilemma and joined in conjuring up pictures of a world from which religious truth is absent. They agreed with each other, notably, in describing the spiritual deformities characteristic of such a world.

When men lose touch with the truth, they become either bigots or infidels. They commit themselves to manifest falsehoods and maintain them fiercely to be true, or find it impossible to settle upon any belief at all. William Ellery Channing, the liberal champion, noted this connection in language his orthodox opponents might easily have adopted: "it is worthy of remark, how nearly the bigot and the skeptic approach. Both . . . throw doubt and confusion over every truth."[8]

These correlative figures bespeak and presuppose a situation in which Calvin's truth, the eternal system ordering human affairs, is overcome by its internal conflicts and breaks into irreconcilable fragments. This is the substance of the relation between Ahab and Ishmael as paired centers of consciousness in *Moby-Dick:* The one displays an "intense bigotry of purpose" (Chap. 36) and the other pursues inconclusive spiritual inquiries and struggles against becoming "a wretched infidel" (Chap. 42). The world of *Moby-Dick* comes to us through these figures, bigotry and skepticism interacting to generate a semantic ground that is inherently unstable, a heaving texture through which the cross pressures and concussions of a religious crisis may be felt.

Melville evokes this Calvinist earthquake so as to portray ultimate reality itself as a zone of tumult; and the engagement with ultimate questions is innately religious, whether traditional practice and doctrine are celebrated or assailed. *Moby-Dick* is in this generic sense a work of religious art; it has the power that Paul Tillich recognized in Picasso's *Guernica,* portraying a shattered reality through which there moves a violent beautiful supernal rhythm.

Moby-Dick is, accordingly, not a dismissal of the biblical and theological traditions it deploys; the sinking of the *Pequod* is not an aquatic version of the one-hoss shay's collapse. On the contrary, Melville challenges us to join a revitalized conversation in which Ahab and Ishmael, Job and Jonah, Solomon and the Man of Sorrows engage the imagination directly, as do the theological conceptions by which religious thinkers in the West had sought to articulate the human traffic with godhead. *Moby-Dick* is a consummate work of religious imagination, standing at the threshold of the modern world and articulating our distinctive religious perplexities; yet the power and authority with which it fashions a modern tradition follows from the mastery with which it brings our ancient inheritance to life.

Ishmael describes the beginning of his spiritual quest in a jocular tone, suggesting that his departure on the whaling voyage came about because of nothing more momentous than a personal whim. "Having little or no money in my purse," he tells us, "and nothing particular to interest me on shore, I thought I would sail about a little and see the watery part of the world" (Chap. 1). This self-deprecating humor, beneath which lurks a notably somber temperament, bespeaks the view of meditative quests that Ishmael's voyage aboard the *Pequod* has led him to adopt. "The key to it all," we are told, is the story of Narcissus, who sought to lay hold of the "ungraspable phantom of life" by plunging into a fountain where he saw his own image reflected. It is the same image, Ishmael tells us, that attracts men universally to undertake voyages into "the watery part of the world," voyages that prove to be an effort to grasp the ungraspable.

Yet the Ishmael who greets us at the outset of *Moby-Dick* has arrived at his present frame of mind by way of the voyage he proposes to recount, and he introduces us to a younger Ishmael who is animated by religious yearnings that have not yet been disavowed. Melville defines the aspirations with which Ishmael begins his voyage by developing an extended comparison of the "land" from which Ishmael departs and the "sea" that he enters, two worlds whose meaning is strongly conditioned by the Calvinistic division of human reality into the realm of the elect and the realm of the reprobate, of "natural man" lost in his sin. To undertake a quest for religious truth, relying on the human capacity for spiritual insight, is to plunge into the domain of the reprobate. Melville invokes the orthodox doctrine that bears on this point in presenting Father Mapple.

Ishmael observes that the preacher is unapproachable in his lofty pulpit after drawing up the rope ladder he uses to ascend it. This "act of physical isolation . . . signifies his spiritual withdrawal . . . from all outward worldly ties and connexions (Chap. 8). Orthodox Calvinists believed that the sacred truths they dispensed from the pulpit were obtained not through human efforts to understand the godhead but from God's own disclosure of himself in the scriptures. The biblical writings had absolute authority precisely because they did not arise from worldly efforts to attain spiritual insight, but embodied God's intention to break through the spiritual darkness surrounding man in his sinful condition. As such, the Bible was an impregnable and all-sufficient resource of divine knowledge: "Yes" Ishmael declares, "for replenished with the meat and wine of the world, to the faithful man of God, this pulpit, I see, is a self-containing stronghold – a lofty Ehrenbreitstein, with a perennial well of waters within the walls."

The scene in Father Mapple's church has a central role in the inauguration of Ishmael's quest, establishing a background of Calvinist doctrine against which Melville plays the religious values that Ishmael finds in his swiftly developing friendship with Queequeg. Ishmael at first responds to Queequeg with abhorrence, his distress aroused by the savage's heathenish idolatry and even more by the prospect of having to sleep with him. Ishmael soon overcomes these misgivings, however, and the transformation of his sentiments amounts to an initiation; it defines the spiritual aspirations with which he enters the "wonder world" of whaling. To us, idolatry and homosexuality may seem quite different things, but to orthodox Calvinists they were closely connected forms of the same perversion.

Men are idolatrous because they do not receive God's revelation in scripture and thus offer worship to objects in the created order rather than to their creator. Not exempted from this condemnation were the ancient Greeks, who had never encountered the Bible, as well as contemporary non-Europeans like Queequeg. They are to blame for their idolatry because the creation itself reinforces the biblical revelation with a revelation of its own, bearing clear evidences of God's true reality. Melville marked in his Bible the passage from St. Paul on which Calvinists grounded this teaching: "For the invisible things of him from the creation of the world are clearly seen, being understood by the things that are made, even his eternal power and Godhead; so that they are without excuse" (Romans 1:19–20).[9] Even though unredeemed men universally fail to see God's manifestations in the created order, they are no less universally at fault. In effect, the signs of the creator are adequate only to place upon men the responsibility for their failure to worship him: "It is not necessary to maintain that this revelation is competent to supply all the knowledge which a sinner needs," a nineteenth-century writer observed. "It is enough that it renders men inexcusable."[10]

Calvinist writers were perfectly aware of the alternative tradition of Christian teaching, which held that pagan philosophers were not totally blinded by sin, but could attain some measure of divine truth by exercising their God-given rationality. This view was the subject of profound meditation in the writings of St. Augustine, was ardently embraced by Christian humanists in the Renaissance (notably in John Milton's commitment to "right reason"), and was adopted with various degrees of emphasis by liberal Christians in the eighteenth and nineteenth centuries. Socrates had a preeminent place in this broad tradition of reverence for the moral rationality of man, having suffered death for the sake of his philosophical vocation. "Holy Socrates," wrote Erasmus, "pray for us."

Yet when nineteenth-century Calvinists surveyed "the character of the heathen," both in the ancient and modern worlds, they observed that heathen conceptions of the deity uniformly distorted the revelation of God in scripture and nature, and also uniformly bore evidence of having been created by men. From the most sophisticated system of religious philosophy to the horrible grinning idols of Polynesia, the objects of non-Christian worship were mere contrivances, products of human activity. Instead of having received God's truth from God, the heathen all "formed their gods after their own imagination."[11]

The act of prostrating oneself in worship before a man-made god is a spiritual perversion, according to Calvinist teaching, that is linked to sexual perversion. Because men "changed the truth of God into a lie," St. Paul asserted, "God gave them up unto vile affections . . . the men, leaving the natural use of the woman, burned in their lust toward one another" (Romans 1:25–7). The orthodox sought to confound the proponents of right reason by lodging this indictment against their Athenian heroes. "The most moral of the Greeks," sneered a Calvinist writer in 1831, "and even the *'martyred Socrates'* practised . . . without shame, abominations which we christians cannot name."[12]

Melville invokes these teachings as he portrays Ishmael returning from Father Mapple's service to find that Queequeg "was holding close up to his face that little negro idol of his; peering hard into its face, and with a jack-knife gently whittling away at its nose, meanwhile humming to himself in his heathenish way." Instead of being disgusted, Ishmael finds a "Socratic wisdom" in the "calm self-collectedness of simplicity" that characterizes his savage friend, and he finds that the ways and worship of Queequeg begin to redeem his own spiritual restlessness. "I felt a melting in me," Ishmael says. "No more my splintered heart and maddened hand were turned against the wolfish world. This soothing savage had redeemed it." Relaxing into an unwonted and deeply welcome intimacy, Ishmael now accepts the signs of friendship offered by the cannibal and enters with him into a marriage that joins them in worship and in bed. "So I kindled the shavings; helped prop up the innocent little idol; offered him burnt biscuit with Queequeg . . . kissed his nose; and that done, we undressed and went to bed. . . . But we did not go to sleep without some little chat. . . . Thus then, in our hearts' honeymoon, lay I and Queequeg – a cosy, loving pair" (Chap. 10).

Ishmael's initiation into the quest thus takes place in circumstances that travesty orthodox belief. The "watery part of the world" is a place where knowledge of the Creator is sought in his creation, yet where exotic forms of worship and forbidden moral relations are embraced for the sake of the truth they may reveal. The practices marked by the orthodox as symbols of man's spiritual blindness are defiantly adopted, becoming symbols of Ishmael's quest for a larger vision of truth, a vision likewise implicit in his relationship to Queequeg. Ishmael refuses to believe that "the magnanimous God of heaven and earth – pagans and all included – can possibly be jealous of an insignificant bit of black wood" (Chap. 10). Instead of a Calvinist monarch who tolerates no rivals, Ishmael envisions a God too generous in spirit to be jealous.

Ishmael sees in Queequeg an embodiment of the religious ideal that he clings to at the outset of the quest, the dream of an encompassing faith that transcends the boundaries separating religious communities. When Captain Bildad tries to find out whether Queequeg has been converted to Christianity, Ishmael replies that Queequeg is a member of the "First Congregational Church," but he does not have in mind the congregationalism that the Puritans brought to New England. He means, instead, "the great and ever-lasting First Congregation of this whole worshipping world; we all belong to that; only some of us cherish some queer crotchets no-ways touching the grand belief; in *that* we all join hands" (Chap. 18).

Ishmael dreams of a truth that is universal, that absorbs what is genuine in the diverse pieties of humankind while refusing to grant a monopoly on religious truth to any of the "queer crotchets" men use to set one system of belief against another. This "democratic faith" asserts that men degrade themselves spiritually not when they fail to receive God's Word but when they form exclusive solidarities that deny the spiritual dignity that is proper to every human creature. "Men may seem detestable as joint stock-companies and nations," Ishmael declares, but in his spiritual essence man is the bearer of a "democratic dignity which, on all hands, radiates without end from God; Himself!" It is man's relation to this "great democratic God" that makes him "so noble and so sparkling, such a grand and glowing creature." "The great God absolute!" Ishmael exclaims, "The centre and circumference of all democracy! His omnipresence, our divine equality!" (Chap. 26).

Ishmael sees Queequeg, and soon comes to see Ahab, as an embodiment of man "in the ideal" through whose spirituality it is possible to glimpse a religious absolute in which he strongly yearns to believe, a God who governs his creation in keeping with human dignity. Yet Ishmael is acutely receptive to circumstances that tend to discredit such a liberal vision. He realizes, for example, that although the dignity of man may be God-given, it can also be destroyed; and he recognizes that "the undraped spectacle of a valor-ruined man" casts doubt upon the proposition that a God respecting human dignity governs human affairs. Ishmael points forward to the fate of Starbuck, and of Ahab, in observing that men may be degraded through circumstances apparently under God's control, so that "piety itself" cannot "completely stifle her upbraidings against the permitting stars" (Chap. 26).

Ishmael's quest persistently tests his central affirmations against circumstances that appear to contradict them. For example, he celebrates Queequeg as a paragon of human dignity, yet also observes that the savage exhibits a bigotry peculiar to his own beliefs. When Ishmael returns from his interview on the *Pequod*, he finds Queequeg in the midst of his Ramadan. Dismayed by the sufferings of the long fast, Ishmael urges Queequeg to recognize that such observances are "stark nonsense; bad for the health; useless for the soul; opposed, in short, to the obvious laws of Hygiene and common sense" (Chap. 17).

Ishmael maintains that a man's religion should not become "a positive torment to him," and that when it "makes this earth of ours an uncomfortable inn to lodge in," it should be modified accordingly. But Queequeg does not believe that religion is meant to serve human well-being; like the orthodox of more familiar persuasions, he regards divine truth as the measure of man, not vice versa. Ishmael concludes that "Queequeg thought he knew a good deal more about the true religion than I did. He looked at me with a sort of condescending concern and compassion, as though he thought it a great pity that such a sensible young man should be so hopelessly lost to evangelical pagan piety" (Chap. 17).

Despite his warm friendship with Queequeg, Ishmael remains quite alone in the flexibility of his religious imagination, his willingness to "cherish the greatest respect for everybody's religious obligations, never mind how comical." He argues that "we good Presbyterian Christians should be charitable in these things, and not fancy ourselves so vastly superior to other mortals, pagans and what not," but not on the ground that the non-Christian religions of the world are innocent of nonsense. On the contrary, he asserts that Queequeg's piety is full of "half-crazy conceits" and "absurd notions." All men may be at one in the impulse to worship, but they are also universally subject to religious folly. "Heaven have mercy on us all – Presbyterians and Pagans alike – for we are all somehow dreadfully cracked about the head, and sadly need mending" (Chap. 17). If there is something genuine in all human worship, there is equally a pervading absurdity in the "somehow dreadfully cracked" religious life of the race.

Instead of a "First Congregation" embracing all mankind, what Ishmael encounters as he makes his way into "the watery part of the world" are figures who represent disparate communities of belief and moral sentiment, and he is attuned to the ironical interplay that takes place when characters like Mapple, Queequeg, Bildad, and Peleg (and later Ahab, Starbuck, and Stubb) respond to one another. Humorous, sympathetic, and chronically distressed, Ishmael makes his way along the boundary lines at which each of these representative individuals maintains a distinctive identity against the others.

This is the substance of Ishmael's own identity as a searcher for religious truth, the meaning Melville sees in his biblical name. The archetypal community of God's elect are the "children of Abraham," meaning the descendants of a son that God promised to Abraham, to be borne by Sarah, Abraham's aged wife. Ishmael was a child born to Hagar, a woman of the household whom Abraham impregnated because he feared that Sarah was too old to conceive. When the child that God had promised finally arrived, Ishmael and Hagar were driven out of the holy family so as to preserve its sacred integrity. Ishmael both was and was not a "child of Abraham"; he occupied an anomalous position on the boundary line separating God's chosen people from the rest of humankind, and thus undermined the religious claim making that boundary absolute.

Melville responded not only to the injustice of Ishmael's fate but also to the systematic spiritual blindness that results from this process of exclusion. Just as systems of collective order maintain their coherence by creating outcasts, so conceptions of religious truth sustain their claim to universal validity by banishing from consideration experiences that pose a threat to the claim.

Melville's way of defining Ishmael's quest includes elements of the now familiar notion that religion is an ideology ratifying social solidarities. Yet, for Melville, the claims of religious truth retained a substantive force; his social insight was acute, but he was not prepared to collapse God's reality into social processes.

These considerations led Melville to the conclusion that a searcher for ultimate truth must take up the role of an outcast, not permitting himself to be ensnared by the self-enclosed havens of religious order that make false claims to universal validity, no matter how comfortable they may be. Melville celebrates this heroic steadfastness in his culminating depiction of the contrast between the sea and the land: The ocean into which Ishmael sets forth is a realm of solitary danger, whereas the land he leaves behind offers comfort and spiritual subservience. "All deep, earnest thinking is but the intrepid effort of the soul to keep the open independence of her sea," Melville proclaims, "while the wildest winds of heaven and earth conspire to cast her on the treacherous, slavish shore." The ocean is also the place of religious reality, where the uncontrollable tumult of a truth beyond all formulation may, for good or ill, be sustained. "But as in landlessness alone resides the highest truth, shoreless, indefinite as God – so, better is it to perish in that howling infinite, than be ingloriously dashed upon the lee, even if that were safety" (Chap. 23).

3

Edward Beecher was troubled by the seemingly intractable debates between liberal and orthodox theologians that proliferated during the early nineteenth century, so he undertook a lengthy course of study to determine why they had not been resolved. In *The Conflict of Ages; or, The Great Debate on the Moral Relations of God and Man* (1853) he identified a fundamental dislocation in Christian theology itself. Liberal Christians he placed in a long tradition celebrating "the principles of honor and right" that affirm human dignity, whereas Calvinists inherited an emphasis upon the "facts of the ruin of man." Beecher asserted that these "main moving powers" had never been reconciled to each other, and that the conflict between them had generated a series of characteristic spiritual quandaries, which he saw reflected in the history of theology, as well as in the doctrinal formulations being argued in his own time. The most extreme and dangerous quandary of all, which arises in a form that no Christian could endorse, Beecher termed "the fifth experience." It was a spiritual state that he considered tantamount to madness. When a conviction of human dignity collides head-on with a recognition of the misery to which human beings are subjected, the resultant moral horrors "present to the mind a malevolent God."[13]

"The fifth experience" is a radical response to the dilemma posed by the earthquake at Lisbon, a challenge to the root axioms by which Calvinism made sense of moral experience. Yet instead of dismissing it as an aberration at the margins of Christian theology, Melville presents Captain Ahab as its embodiment.

Liberal and orthodox traditions of religious understanding, so deeply at odds as to fuel centuries of bitter conflict, are forced by Melville into a single dramatic framework at whose heart is a madman obsessed by the vision of a malevolent God. Ishmael's dream of a liberal religion establishes the premise that he uses to gauge the character and experience of Ahab; and Ahab himself takes his stand, at least at the outset, upon the dignity of man. Yet what actually happens to Ahab conforms to the orthodox description of God's dealings with a fallen human race.

The jarring conjunctions of these antagonistic religious perspectives meet us at every stage of Ahab's story; his madness becomes the incoherence of religious meaning itself, as generated in Calvinist culture. Melville invokes from time to time the cognitive refinements of theological debate, but the heart of his narrative rests upon classic motifs of Calvinism as a living faith, in particular the experience of conversion, through which a sinner is rescued by God from his innate depravity and transformed into an obedient servant. Father Mapple's sermon on Jonah, which describes this process, anchors the presentation of Ahab's doom.

The Calvinist God does not make converts by appealing to man's reason and moral sense; on the contrary, a sinner must be brought to violate the dictates of his fallen nature. "If we obey God," Mapple explains, "we must disobey ourselves; and it is in this disobeying ourselves, wherein the hardness of obeying God consists" (Chap. 9).

In the evangelical tradition of Calvinist pietism, disobeying oneself involved becoming a new person altogether, in a spiritual "rebirth" whose stages were outlined in Philip Doddridge's *The Rise and Progress of Religion in the Soul*. Doddridge traced a process of spiritual regeneration in which the sinner is "awakened," "sentenced," "struck with the terror of his sentence," and then receives "news of salvation."[14] This is the pattern Father Mapple sees in Jonah's experience; he declares it to be "a story of the sin, hard-heartedness, suddenly awakened fears, the swift punishment, repentance, prayers, and finally the deliverance and joy of

124

Jonah" (Chap. 9). Jonah is mangled by guilt as he boards the ship for Tarshish, in disobedience of God's command, but he does not truly repent even when the sailors throw him overboard to quiet the storm God sends. The full terror takes hold only when God comes upon Jonah in the whale.

Orthodox tradition invoked the awesome strength and presumed ferocity of the whale as a symbol for the wrath of God. In the famous retort by which God had silenced the rebellious questionings of Job, Leviathan was invoked as a manifestation of divine anger aroused by human impudence. Calvin published sixty-five sermons on the Book of Job, and in the tradition he established, the Leviathan was typically identified with the whale. God "can destroy us, sooner than Leviathan can crush us, were we between his teeth. The consideration of the terribleness that is in any Creature; should lead us to consider how terrible the Lord is to those who provoke him. Are the teeth of a Leviathan . . . terrible? . . . How terrible then is the wrath of God!"[15]

When this terror is aimed at the sinner's redemption, he recognizes that God has been righteous in his dreadful inflictions. The sinner must loathe himself for his moral condition, just as God loathes him, as a precondition to recognizing the unmerited love God displays in choosing to redeem him. As sinful men, we must "be willing to own the vengeance of Almighty God, and to judge ourselves, to justify him that may condemn us, and be witnesses against ourselves."[16] Father Mapple accordingly celebrates Jonah's eventual submission: "Jonah does not weep and wail for direct deliverance. He feels that his dreadful punishment is just. . . . And here, shipmates, is true and faithful repentence; not clamorous for pardon, but grateful for punishment. And how pleasing to God was this conduct in Jonah, is shown in the eventual deliverance of him from the sea and the whale" (Chap. 9).

Melville develops an elaborate antithesis between the submission of Jonah and the defiance of Captain Ahab. Jonah accepts the whale's attack as a divine correction; Ahab takes it as an outrageous affront. Jonah yields to the divine assault in terror; Ahab resists it in fury. Jonah moves on to do his Lord's bidding; Ahab sets out upon an "audacious, immitigable, and supernatural revenge." Seeing in Moby Dick's attack an effort to silence his own

125

rebellious challenge to God's justice, Ahab devotes himself to "chasing with curses a Job's whale round the world" (Chap. 41).

The drama of salvation that Mapple describes had a traditional counterpart in orthodox teaching, namely, the hellish conflict between Calvin's God and the reprobate, of which the Old Testament story of King Ahab provided an example. Thomas Robinson's *Scripture Characters,* an early nineteenth-century orthodox commentary for use in families, explains that although the sacred records "relate chiefly to those who were 'redeemed,'" they also bring before us examples of "our nature in a state of awful degeneracy." King Ahab is presented as "a sinner of peculiar infamy, depraved beyond the common measure of his species."[17]

Robinson observes that King Ahab persists in his wickedness despite the punishments God inflicted upon him, which shows that God's saving grace is not at work in his heart. "Some bold offenders become the more obdurate under the divine corrections. Such is the hardness and impenitence of the human heart, that neither mercies or judgments will of themselves, soften or subdue it."[18] The reprobate cannot repent because God has not ordained that he should; but God nonetheless punishes him, and the result is typically an escalation of punishment and furious rebellion, such as took place in the ten plagues of Egypt: "What desperate and horrible rage did the heart of Pharoah swell into, when, in the midst of those fearful judgments, he hardened his heart, and exalted himself."[19]

Calvinist writers recognized that reprobate fury might be triggered by a "natural" affliction, such as the attack of a wild animal, stirring a man to anger against the God who had ordained it. They insisted that such anger should be turned against the self to bring about repentance. "Do not repine at God's providence, nor quarrel with the dumb creatures; but let thine indignation reflect upon thine own heart."[20] After Ahab reveals to the crew that he is seeking revenge, Starbuck objects in terms that invoke this admonition: "To be enraged with a dumb thing . . . seems blasphemous." To which Ahab frantically replies, "Talk not to me of blasphemy, man; I'd strike the sun if it insulted me" (Chap. 36).

Ahab sees divine malice in the attack of the whale, the malice that Calvin's God directs against those whom he does not choose to redeem, yet Ahab's own vengeful hatred is itself evidence that God's wrath is at work. The fate of the reprobate, in Calvinist teaching, is to sustain a horrible existence — in this world and the next — that is characterized by reciprocal hatred, God hating the sinner as the sinner hates God. This situation is ordained by a decree that Calvin himself termed "dreadful," God's determination that Adam should fall and that his sin should extend to the entire human race.[21] To Ahab, as to liberal critics of Calvin, this teaching evoked a divine monster ruthlessly violating the central principles of moral truth.

Yet to Ahab it was not a matter of doctrine but of manifest reality. The monster was real; it had assaulted him; and he saw in it "that intangible malignity which has been from the beginning; to whose dominion even the modern Christians ascribe one-half of the worlds." Ahab enacts in his pursuit of Moby Dick the frenzy of mutual rage that God had ordained from the foundations of the earth. "He piled upon the whale's white hump all the general rage and hate felt by his whole race from Adam down" (Chap. 41).

Orthodox teachers found that the spiritual blindness of sinful men was most likely to reveal itself on just this issue. Calvin frankly admitted that he was unable to explain how God could decree the fall of Adam without becoming the "author of sin," and he took this incapacity as dazzling evidence of God's glory: "why should we wonder that the *infinite* and incomprehensible majesty of God should surpass the narrow limits of our *finite* intellect?" If men in their deluded pride of reason perceive God's providence as unjust, they only demonstrate how unfit they are to take up spiritual questions that challenge the revealed truth. "Those who seek to know more than God has revealed," Calvin asserted, "are *madmen*!"[22]

Ahab has in himself something more than madness; he not only accuses God of injustice but passes beyond accusation to the "madness maddened" of revenge, seeking to "dismember my dismemberer." And the ultimate target of Ahab's assault is the "incomprehensible majesty" that Calvin had invoked in defending God's justice. "I see in him outrageous strength," Ahab proclaims, "with an inscrutable malice sinewing it. That inscrutable thing is chiefly what I hate" (Chap. 36). Ahab conceives the "reasoning thing" behind the objects of experience to be shielded by a "mask" no tougher than "pasteboard," and carries out a plunging intellectual attack, like the darting of his harpoon, in order to "strike through the mask" and liberate himself from subjection to the divine mystery. If Ahab has his way with Moby Dick, that presumptive sign and vehicle of God's secret decree, nothing will remain but a dead whale.

To William Ellery Channing, religious reality testified to the dignity of man. "Should the whole order and purposes of the universe be opened to us," he affirmed, "it is certain that nothing would be disclosed that would in any degree shake our persuasion, that the world is inhabited by rational and moral beings who are authorized to expect from their creator the most benevolent and equitable government" (Vol. 3, p. 228). This teaching, which Channing was able to articulate with such consummate serenity, is a subject of convulsive frenzy in Ahab's character, and his battle with the dread powers involves moral contradictions unimagined in Channing's rationalism.

Ahab condemns the divine violence embodied in Moby Dick on the ground that men "are authorized" to demand an "equitable government" from the Creator. Yet the obsessive hatred and fury of his revolt manifest the depravity that Calvin saw as innate to human nature. Melville thus discredits both religious stances: He sets forth a Calvinistic analysis of Ahab's moral strife in order to form a drama in which Calvin's God appears morally odious on liberal principles, yet in which liberal principles lose their validity as a description of religious truth. Ahab's character encloses a turbulence in which orthodox belief and Channing's "persuasion" are broken against each other.

Melville deploys these warring traditions so as to enhance Ahab's spiritual magnitude, his presence as a "mighty pageant creature" capable of sustaining tragic conflicts that would shatter the character of a lesser man. Ahab's relation to Fedallah ennobles him in just this fashion, as a transformation of Calvin's teaching on the role of Satan in the life of the damned.

Calvin found the Old Testament story of Ahab especially useful because it illustrated God's control of Satan and demonstrated that God's ordering of the creation through providence is indeed exhaustive. God wants Ahab to set out on a suicidal military adventure, so he appoints Satan to induce him to do so. "God sends Satan to Ahab, with his own Divine command that he should be 'a lying spirit in the mouth of all the king's prophets.' Thus the imposter spirit becomes the minister of the wrath of God, to blind the wicked."[23] Melville inverts this Calvinist teaching in presenting Fedallah: "Ahab seemed an independent lord; the Parsee but his slave. Still again both seemed yoked together, and an unseen tyrant driving them" (Chap. 130). Melville invokes liberal principle when he terms Fedallah the agent of an "unseen tyrant" rather than the minister of a holy God who does not share the evil of the errand on which he sends Satan.

But Melville declares also that Fedallah is a projection of Ahab's own self-determining purpose, so that the presumptive Calvinistic divine tyrant is fused with a dynamism internal to Ahab himself that is the essence of his personhood. At the core of Ahab's being is not free will guided by rational morality but a paradoxical agony in which Ahab's freedom and his tragic destiny are both antithetical and at one. Melville presents Ahab and Fedallah "fixedly gazing upon each other; as if in the Parsee Ahab saw his forethrown shadow, in Ahab the Parsee his abandoned substance." This peculiar divorce of shadow and substance, and the suggestions of divine overruling, actually complete Ahab's truest nature rather than violating it: "For be this Parsee what he may, all rib and keel was solid Ahab" (Chap. 130).

Melville further dramatizes Ahab's paradoxical inner state by exploiting orthodox descriptions of the ravages of sin. Man's nature is depraved, Calvinists taught, but he nonetheless finds a wonderful fulfillment when God chooses to redeem him. This comes about because human beings still have remnants of an original virtue, God's image in man as created before the Fall, which survives in a marred and diminished form under the subjugation of sin. As John Owen's *Indwelling Sin* explained, the power of sin "appears in the violence it offers to the nature of men, compelling them to sins, fully contrary to . . . the reasonable nature wherewith they are endued from God."[24] Correspondingly, Melville says that Ahab's "great natural intellect" had been the "living agent" in him before his injury, but then became the instrument of his madness. Ahab's madness is a usurping tyrant that "stormed his general sanity, and carried it, and turned all its concentred cannon upon its own mad mark" (Chap. 41).

Thus in sleep Ahab's rational soul struggled to break free from the mad purpose that had forced it into servitude: "it spontaneously sought escape from the scorching contiguity of the frantic thing, of which, for the time, it was no longer an integral." Ahab's purpose had "by its own sheer inveteracy of will, forced itself against gods and devils into a kind of self-assumed, independent being of its own. Nay, could grimly live and burn, while the common vitality to which it was conjoined, fled horror-stricken from the unbidden and unfathered birth." Owen declared that the mind of the sinner "is, as it were, the upper region of hell; for it lies at the next door to it for filth, horror, and confusion."[25] Ahab's soul is just such a scene of torment: "a chasm seemed opening in him, from which forced flames and lightnings shot up, and accursed fiends beckoned him to leap down among them; when this hell in himself yawned beneath him, a wild cry would be heard through the ship" (Chap. 44).

Ahab is delivered from this internal chaos through ecstatic union with the divine, which Melville portrays by inverting the fulfillment that the elect enjoy when they are redeemed. When one of God's chosen is reborn, he is enabled by grace to serve his creator with a whole heart. Father Mapple himself, like the Jonah of his sermon, exemplifies this fulfillment: He deploys the energies of "his own inexorable self" in declaring his submission to the dispensations of the Almighty.

In "The Candles," Ahab stands before the masts of the *Pequod,* with their "trinity of flames." "I own thy speechless, placeless power; but to the last gasp of my earthquake life will dispute its unconditional, unintegral mastery in me . . . while I earthly live, the queenly personality lives in me, and feels her royal rights" (Chap. 119). The personality has royal status, according to liberal Christian theory, because men have an inherent right to question the justice of whatever divine power demands worshipful submission. There is "a principle within us," William Ellery Channing declared, "which forbids us to prostrate ourselves before mere power" (Vol. 1, p. 232). Thus Ahab addresses the spirit in the flame: "Come in thy lowest form of love, and I will kneel and kiss thee; but . . . come as mere supernal power; and . . . there's that in here that still remains indifferent" (Chap. 119).

Ahab cannot offer the worship of submission; he seizes, instead, a worship Channing did not envision. If God unjustly creates rebellious beings only to destroy them, those beings may offer him a worship suitable to their fate. "To neither love nor reverence wilt thou be kind; and e'en for hate thou canst but kill; and all are killed." Therefore Ahab achieves the truest and deepest expression of his own being by coming to the furious conviction that for him "right worship is defiance." In that worship he can join the hell fire in himself with the confirming and answering hell fire of rage that he finds arrayed against him, and so pursue objectives that are most truly his own and at once harmonious with the ultimate context in which his life is set. "Oh, thou clear spirit, of thy fire thou madest me, and like a true child of fire, I breathe it back to thee." Whereas the member of the elect finds the freedom of his own truest life in obedience to the divine decrees, the reprobate finds his deepest fulfillment in the defiance that has been decreed for him. Thus Ahab celebrates his unification with the divine: "I leap with thee; I burn with thee; would fain be welded with thee; defyingly I worship thee!" (Chap. 119).

Ahab struggles to maintain this demoniac integrity as his quest approaches its final climax, and he begins to act out William Ellery Channing's assertion that "the God of Calvinism, if made a model for human conduct, would turn men into monsters" (Vol. 1, p. 238). Critical discussions of *Moby-Dick* have generally recognized that Ahab retains something of his "humanities": His capacity for loyalty and affection and his sense of fair play continue to assert themselves. Yet, as is equally well recognized, he becomes a contemptuous tyrant in relation to his crew; and the culmination of his quest, for all its cosmic heroism, simply wastes their lives. He becomes himself an agent of the divine evil that he hates.

Ahab's fate, and Ishmael's response to it, raise the central question: Can any credible conception of the godhead provide a model for human conduct? This question strikes at the heart of the Calvinist tradition as it descended from the sixteenth century, that composite of internal tensions that prompted Arminius's challenge and Milton's great vindication, generated a broad spectrum of views in the eighteenth century, and embraced liberal and orthodox believers in Melville's own time. The tradition rested upon two great axioms: that God's will governs the world he has created, such that a true understanding of what happens in the world reveals his nature; and second, that the divine nature thus revealed is the essence of justice, having absolute authority over human affairs. In *Moby-Dick* Melville sets these axioms at odds.

Ahab's "earthquake life" speaks directly to Ishmael's religious consternations, the difficulties he encounters in trying to confirm his belief in a "great democratic God." For a time Ishmael commits himself to Ahab's quest, but then moves on to articulate a religious consciousness emerging amid the wreckage of the Calvinist tradition.

4

In explaining why "Ahab's quenchless feud seemed mine," Ishmael does not recount additional examples of the wanton destructiveness of whales and other vicious creatures of God; he records instead his response to a treachery that seems to arise from the creation as a whole. The whiteness of Moby Dick arouses a special dread and fury in Ishmael, sentiments that he believes all men share:

> Is it that by its indefiniteness it shadows forth the heartless voids and immensities of the universe, and thus stabs us from behind with the thought of annihilation . . . ? Or is it, that as in essence whiteness is not so much a color as the visible absence of color, and at the same time the concrete of all colors; is it for these reasons that there is such a dumb blankness, full of meaning, in a wide landscape of snows – a colorless, all-color of atheism from which we shrink? And when we consider that other theory of the natural philosophers, that all other earthly hues – every stately or lovely emblazoning . . . all these are but subtile deceits, not actually inherent in substances, but only laid on from without; so that all deified Nature absolutely paints like the harlot, whose allurements cover nothing but the charnel-house within; and when we . . . consider that . . . the great principle of light, for ever remains white or colorless in

132

itself, and if operating without medium upon matter, would touch all objects, even tulips and roses, with its own blank tinge – pondering all this, the palsied universe lies before us a leper" (Chap. 42).

The images of the harlot, the charnel-house, and the leper register Ishmael's horror and disgust at a spiritual failure he cannot blame on himself, the failure of his effort to discern a spiritual reality worthy of worship by looking upon the universe as a symbolic articulation of God's character. Instead of a creation grounded in the deity, the world now appears a vast blank. Yet as this realization dawns upon the searcher for truth, he takes it as an act of cosmic treachery against himself, in which an inherently godless nature has somehow been "deified" by qualities that are not inherent, but only applied like rouge and lipstick to deceive him. The "wonder-world" of spiritual meditation had beckoned with exotic beauty, and had promised an enlarged realization of truth in which the transcendent meanings of earthly experience coalesce into a magnanimous vision of the godhead. In the betrayal of this promise, the quester himself is degraded: The powers of religious insight that he has cultivated – as the part of his own nature attuned to intimations of the divine nature – are annihilated even as the religious depth of the visible world is found to be a void. The searcher after truth becomes a "wretched infidel [who] gazes himself blind" (Chap. 42).

Yet Ishmael does not finally adopt the radically diminished conception of himself and the world that impels him to join Ahab in seeking cosmic revenge. The fact that Ahab is a "monomaniac" at length comes home to Ishmael: He realizes that Ahab's conception of reality is as one-sided as any scheme of divine benevolence. Invoking the demented religious integrity Ahab achieves through the "spirit of fire," Ishmael declares his repudiation: "Give not thyself up to the fire, lest it invert thee, deaden thee; as for the time it did me" (Chap. 96). If believers who ascribe benevolence to God are placed in a hopeless quandary by the "problem of evil," then old Ahab's mad faith in a malevolent God is discredited by a corresponding "problem of good."

Ishmael does not claim to have discovered a system of religious belief within which Ahab's indictment of divine malevolence can be digested. He simply observes that Ahab's piety causes him to see religious reality only in scenes of horror, whereas scenes of bliss turn to bitterness in his sight. Ishmael himself, by contrast, sees both the horror of the ocean and its moments of transfigured gentleness:

> The long-drawn virgin vales; the mild blue hill-sides; as over these there steals the hush, the hum; you almost swear that play-wearied children lie sleeping in these solitudes, in some glad May-time, when the flowers of the woods are plucked. And all this mixes with your most mystic mood; so that fact and fancy, half-way meeting, interpenetrate, and form one seamless whole.
>
> Nor did such soothing scenes, however temporary, fail of at least as temporary an effect on Ahab. But if these secret golden keys did seem to open in him his own secret golden treasuries, yet did his breath upon them prove but tarnishing (Chap. 114).

Ishmael is capable of moments of ecstatic consciousness in which, like Ahab, he apprehends the universe as a realm of evil. But he also has religious experiences in which the whole of things is envisioned as joyous and loving.

Writing to Hawthorne in the final stages of his work on *Moby-Dick*, Melville comments on the vicissitudes of ecstatic consciousness in terms that illuminate his way of handling this issue. He scoffs at Goethe's belief that the torments of life can be eliminated if one will *"Live in the all."* A man with a raging toothache would not likely be mollified by being told to feel "the tinglings of life that are felt in the flowers and . . . the Fixed Stars." On the contrary, as Melville's treatment of Ahab demonstrates, acute personal suffering can yield a malignant vision of the "all," as compelling in its moments of intensity as any transcendental joy. This awareness does not lead Melville to the conclusion that the "all feeling" yields no insight into the nature of reality, but persuades him that it yields only a partial insight. "What plays the mischief with the truth," he asserts, "is that men will insist upon the universal application of a temporary feeling or opinion."[26] Melville does not reject Goethe's maxim on the ground of mundane common sense; nor does he reject it because his own powers of mystical consciousness are weak. It is the prodigality with which he can evoke such moments of ecstatic awareness that leads him to reckon with the significance of their variety.

Through Ishmael, Melville presents the major characters of his tale as having mutually discrepant spiritual integrities. Queequeg, Father Mapple, and Ahab each has a distinctive selfhood that is sealed to a distinctive vision of religious reality in moments of ecstatic consciousness. The service in the whaleman's chapel, Queequeg's Ramadan, and Ahab's "worship of defiance" are all moments in which rituals are performed, consummating diverse conceptions of ultimate reality. A comparable observation can be made regarding individual chapters in *Moby-Dick*, where Ishmael engages in meditations that rise from the practical details of the whale hunt to create a symbolic encounter with the transcendent. These meditations lead notably individualized lives, such that critical efforts to draw them together into a comprehensive thematic harmony have always foundered. "What is the meaning of the White Whale?" is now a threadbare academic joke; it is a question to which there is no answer, one that has called forth countless replies.

Yet the prime target of the joke is not explainers of literary texts in the twentieth century, but our forebears in the nineteenth century whose province was a majestic sacred text in two books: The first book was God's Word in scripture; the second was his Word in the creation. Taken together these books were thought to encode a logically unified and intelligible body of truth having supreme moral authority over human society in all times and places. Edward Beecher explained how this almighty apparatus was supposed to work as he watched it breaking down in 1853. "We need a system that shall give us the power intelligently to meet and logically to solve all of the great religious and social problems that we are called on to encounter in the great work of converting the world, and thoroughly reorganizing human society."[27]

A parody of such ambitions is presented in Ishmael's comment on the tattoos of Queequeg, which are at length revealed as a work of theology, "a complete theory of the heavens and the earth, and a mystical treatise on the art of attaining truth." But it is a treatise that no one can read, so that "these mysteries were . . . destined in the end to moulder away with the living parchment whereon they were inscribed, and so be unsolved to the last" (Chap. 110). Ishmael's joke blandly leads to anguish as he asks, what sane coherence is possible in a world where religious meanings are not only disparate but also perishable?

Queequeg's tattooing is one of several figures in which Ishmael considers the possibility of weaving an intelligible pattern from the diverse truths of his experience. Freedom, fate, and chance are interwoven in "The Mat-Maker"; life and death are interwoven in "A Bower of the Arsacides"; fact and fancy "form one seamless whole" in "The Glider," where a moment of spiritual confidence yields to the grim conclusion that the secret of man's paternity is hidden in the grave: the interweaving of life's source with its end. This deep texture, the interweaving of life and death, preoccupies Ishmael from the opening sentences of the book: Queequeg's undecipherable tattoo, transferred from his living body to the coffin that then becomes a life buoy, is complicated and recomplicated as a symbol for this profoundest secret of experience. But it conveys, finally, its own inscrutability; Melville develops the image so as to body forth the unreadable.

We have observed that the tradition of controversy regarding Calvinist theology featured extended discussions of the mystery of the godhead. John Toland's famous *Christianity Not Mysterious* (1696) proclaimed the classic deist challenge on this issue, and William Ellery Channing represents one version of the liberal Christian claim that the Calvinists were wrong to represent God as altogether beyond human understanding. Calvinist orthodoxy, by contrast, must be recognized as having preserved a vision of this tragic dimension of human experience, where suffering and ruin are incomprehensibly severe. Yet the orthodox insistence on the inscrutable character of God's providence came increasingly to act as a defensive maneuver protecting key positions in a theological system that was famous for its inexorable logic. It is one thing to invoke the divine mystery in order to secure a one-hoss shay of rational order; it is quite another to experience religious reality itself as unaccountable.

This difference is figured in the contrast that finally emerges between Ahab's vision of the whale and that of Ishmael. Ahab visualizes the whale with increasing clarity as a monster embodying the features of Calvin's God as they appear hateful on liberal principles. In the description of Moby Dick's final attack, the famous tenets are all there: predestination, retribution, and the helplessness of mortal men before the divine dispensations. Moby Dick "from side to side strangely vibrating his predestinating head, sent a broad band of overspreading semicircular foam before him as he rushed. Retribution, swift vengeance, eternal malice were in his whole aspect, and spite of all that mortal man could do, the solid white buttress of his forehead smote the ship's starboard bow, till men and timbers reeled" (Chap. 135).

Ishmael's vision of the whale is a manifold of visions, among which fresh resonances can be detected so long as spirit and strength permit the reader to keep listening for them. Ishmael also sees the whale as a symbol of God, even of the supreme God, yet with a consciousness of mystery arising instantly, in moment after moment.

> If hereafter any highly cultured, poetical nation shall lure back to their birth-right, the merry May-day gods of old; and livingly enthrone them again in the now egotistical sky; on the now unhaunted hill; then be sure, exalted to Jove's high seat, the great Sperm Whale shall lord it.
>
> Campollion deciphered the wrinkled granite hieroglyphics. But there is no Champollion to decipher the Egypt of every man's and every being's face. Physiognomy, like every other human science, is but a passing fable. If then, Sir William Jones, who read in thirty languages, could not read the simplest peasant's face in its profounder and more subtle meanings, how may unlettered Ishmael hope to read the awful Chaldee of the Sperm Whale's brow? I but put that brow before you. Read it if you can. (Chap. 79)

This evocation of the unreadable divine is not presented to safeguard a theological system. It celebrates a fullness virtually beyond imagining, in which the myriad commonplace details of ordinary experience are charged with sacred mystery, every man's and every being's face alive with meanings that explanation may illuminate, but never exhaust.

Melville delivers this living mystery not by engaging our imagination in a stable thematic or symbolic structure. We find here no self-contained organic unity of the sort the old New Criticism looked upon as the criterion of artistic merit. Nor does Melville posit such coherence as the sine qua non of meaning itself, and by undermining that coherence celebrate a void, or a spurious voice within the void ceaselessly reiterating its own spuriousness. Melville is not a man who means no meanings.

His art invokes opposed perspectives simultaneously, establishes vehement thematic premises and then reverses them, fuses horror with mildness and self-destruction with apotheosis. His home ground is the intergrading of opposites: the frozen tensions, sudden bucklings, and massive slow friction that arise where the stone plates undergirding the lands and the seas grind against each other. Yet it is not these dislocations themselves that preoccupy Melville finally, but the deeper reality they disclose. He was aware that the Bible and other religious scripture, like the best of theological writing, point beyond themselves to a living mystery at the limits of human understanding. Melville's immense theological and biblical learning is deployed in *Moby-Dick* to fashion a discourse remaining true to the spiritual boundary where received forms of understanding break down and new possibilities become available, yet where new forms of understanding, once attained, only multiply the avenues by which the religious imagination arrives once again at the unknown. It is finally the life of such an imagination, the agony and delight that are native to its life, that Melville summons us to share in *Moby-Dick*.

NOTES

1. Miriam Rossiter Small, *Oliver Wendell Holmes* (New York: Twayne Publishers, 1962) p. 99.
2. Clifford Geertz, "Religion as a Cultural System," in *The Interpretation of Cultures* (New York: Basic Books, 1973); Peter Berger, *The Sacred Canopy* (Garden City, N.Y.: Doubleday, 1967).
3. John Calvin, *Calvin's Calvinism*, trans. Henry Cole (Grand Rapids, Mich.: W. B. Eerdmans Pub. Co., 1950), p. 189.
4. Max Weber, *The Protestant Ethic and the Spirit of Capitalism*, trans. Talcott Parsons (New York: Scribner, 1958); Michael Walzer, *The Revolution of the Saints: A Study in the Origins of Radical Politics* (New

York: Atheneum, 1973); Keith Thomas, *Religion and the Decline of Magic* (New York: Scribner, 1971); David Little, *Religion, Order and and Law: A Study in Pre-Revolutionary England* (New York: Harper Torchbooks, 1969); E. P. Thompson, "Time, Work-Discipline, and Industrial Capitalism," *Past and Present* 38 (Dec. 1967): 56–97.

5. See Author's Preface and "The Lisbon Earthquake," in *The Works of Voltaire*, trans. William F. Fleming, 22 vols (New York: The St. Hubert Guild, 1901), vol. 10, pp. 5–10. For the attendant controversy, see Georg Brandes, *Voltaire* (New York: Tudor Publishing Co., 1930), pp. 88–9.

6. Quoted in John Taylor, *The Scripture Doctrine of Original Sin, Proposed to a Free and Candid Examination* (London: J. Wilson, 1740, *Supplement*, 1741), p. 43. Taylor's *Scripture Doctrine* was an anti-Calvinist classic that Melville had at hand when he was writing *Moby-Dick*. See Merton M. Sealts, Jr., *Melville's Reading: A Checklist of Books Owned and Borrowed* (Madison, Wis.: The University of Wisconsin Press, 1966), p. 98.

7. See the Bibliography for information about the text of *Moby-Dick* cited in this chapter.

8. William Ellery Channing, *Works*, 6 vols. (Boston: George G. Channing, 1849), Vol. 3, p. 66. Subsequent references to this edition will appear in the text.

9. *The New Testament . . . The Book of Psalms* (New York: American Bible Society, 1844). See Sealts, *Melville's Reading*, No. 65.

10. Charles Hodge, *A Commentary on the Epistle to the Romans* (1836; rpt. Philadelphia: H. Perkins, 1870), p. 34.

11. "The Character of the Heathen," *Magazine of the Dutch Church* 4 (1931):333–40.

12. Ibid., p. 339.

13. Edward Beecher, *The Conflict of Ages; or, The Great Debate on the Moral Relations of God and Man* (Boston: Phillips, Sampson & Company, 1854), pp. 184–91. Subsequent references to this edition will appear in the text.

14. Philip Doddridge, *The Rise and Progress of Religion in the Soul* (New York: American Tract Society, n.d.) The terms quoted are in the table of contents.

15. Joseph Caryl, *An Exposition with Practical Observations upon the Book of Job*, 2 vols. (London: Samuel Simmons, 1676–7), vol. 2, p. 2249.

16. Edward Reynolds, *Works*, 6 vols. (London: B. Riveley, 1826), vol. 1, p. 111.

17. Thomas Robinson, *Scripture Characters, or a Practical Improvement of the Principal Histories in the Old and New Testaments*, 4 vols. (London: J. Mathews 1808) vol. 2, p. 240.
18. Ibid., p. 244.
19. Reynolds, *Works*, vol. 1, p. 158.
20. Ibid., p. 76.
21. John Calvin, *Institutes of the Christian Religion*, ed. John T. McNeill, trans. F. L. Battles, 2 vols. (Philadelphia: The Westminster Press, 1960), vol. 2, p. 955.
22. Calvin, *Calvin's Calvinism*, pp. 126–7.
23. Ibid., p. 240.
24. John Owen, *The Nature, Power, Deceit and Prevalency of Indwelling Sin in Believers* (Philadelphia: The Presbyterian Board of Governors, n.d.), pp. 245–6. See also James Tanis, *Dutch Calvinist Pietism in the Middle Colonies: A Study in the Life and Theology of Theodorus Jacobus Frelinghuysen* (The Hague: Martinus Nijhoff, 1967), p. 104.
25. Ibid., p. 171.
26. Herman Melville, *The Letters of Herman Melville*, ed. Merrell R. Davis and William H. Gilman (New Haven, Conn.: Yale University Press, 1960), pp. 130–1.
27. Beecher, *The Conflict of Ages*, p. iii.

When Is a Painting Most Like a Whale?: Ishmael, *Moby-Dick*, and the Sublime

BRYAN WOLF

O N October 6, 1847, the young Herman Melville, newly arrived upon the New York literary scene, attended the opening night celebration of the Art Union. The Art Union, which
represented virtually every aspiring American painter of the period, had moved to new quarters on Broadway, and Melville, together with his publisher and mentor, Evert Duyckinck, joined at
least "five hundred invited guests" who sampled the art and the
fine wine that accompanied it. Among the many "clergymen, literary men, editors and artists" present, Melville met William
Cullen Bryant, dean of American nature poets, and William
Sidney Mount, a leading genre painter of the period.

Two years later, Bryant reappeared as a figure in a painting
undoubtedly seen by Melville, Asher B. Durand's *Kindred Spirits*
(Fig. 1). The painting is a memorial tribute to Thomas Cole, father
of the Hudson River school of landscape art. Cole had died unexpectedly in 1848, and Durand eulogized the painter by placing him
next to Bryant in an imaginary Catskill landscape. The title of the
painting, together with its forested vistas, reminds us how close
painters and writers were to each other in the early nineteenth
century. They were linked by many common circumstances: They
shared a spirit of artistic nationalism and believed themselves capable of catapulting America into the vanguard of Western culture. They viewed the American wilderness with a complicated
spectrum of emotions ranging from pride to trepidation. When
they were not engaged in exploring the landscape in their art or
their writings, they engaged each other in endless hours of conversation, camaraderie, and occasional rivalry.

What Melville carried away from his acquaintance with American painting we can only surmise. As a disillusioned writer a decade later, Melville commenced his journey to the Holy Land with a stop in London, where he spent an afternoon at the Dulwich Gallery admiring the "gems" he found there: "Titians, Claudes, Salvators, [and] Murillos." Later in his life, he was presented with a copy of James Jackson Jarves's *The Art Idea*. He underscored the passage that describes Washington Allston, America's first full-fledged romantic painter, as a discouraged old man struggling against a philistine culture.

What is more certain than scattered biographical details is that Melville felt the pressure of landscape art in his own writing. In the "Sunset" chapter of *Moby-Dick*, Ahab responds to the prospect of sea and sky before him as if it were a Hudson River school vista. His view of the horizon is framed by his cabin window, where he sits alone, indoors, observing the sun in its slow decline to the west:

> Yonder, by the ever-brimming goblet's rim, the warm waves blush like wine. The gold brow plumbs the blue. The diver sun – slow dived from noon, goes down; my soul mounts up! (Chap. 37)

Two years later, in a short story entitled "Bartleby the Scrivener," Melville again described a landscape with language borrowed from the world of art. The scene this time is an urban vista rather than a sea view; it is framed by a window and illuminated by "a spacious sky-light shaft, penetrating the building from top to bottom."

> This view might have been considered rather tame than otherwise, deficient in what landscape painters call "life." But, if so, the view from the other end of my chambers offered, at least, a contrast, if nothing more. In that direction, my windows commanded an unobstructed view of a lofty brick wall, black by age and everlasting shade; which wall required no spy-glass to bring out its lurking beauties, but for the benefit of all near-sighted spectators, was pushed up to within ten feet of my window panes.[1]

Despite the contrasting settings of these two descriptions, the manner of vision is the same. Nature, or whatever substitutes for it, is composed according to conventions derived from the visual arts.

The reference to the "spy-glass" not only mocks the lack of an appropriate landscape vista but refers historically to the once popular practice of viewing large-scale landscape canvases with operatic glasses in specially lighted exhibition halls.

Melville's practice of putting nature behind a frame suggests that he was more interested in the framing than in the landscape. And indeed, his language bears out this point. The passage from "Bartleby" focuses on the viewer's act of perception rather than the view itself: The imagery of spy-glasses and spectators emphasizes the role of the observer. So too in the "Sunset" chapter of *Moby-Dick*, nature is not only converted into a painting and held in abeyance by a frame, it literally disappears. As the sun goes down, Ahab's "soul mounts up," replacing nature's powers with his own.

This voiding of the sun helps explain the black brick wall blocking the vista in the offices of the narrator of "Bartleby the Scrivener." Nature has disappeared in "Bartleby"; it is present only through Melvilles's many ironic allusions to its absence. We may assume that its demise owes something to the story's setting: the commercial world of mid-nineteenth-century Wall Street. Nature and the tradition of agrarian values symbolized by landscape art have been replaced by the economies and perspectives of urban finance.

But we know from the "Sunset" chapter that nature vanished as anything more than an artistic convention long before Bartleby entered the world of Wall Street. Its eclipse began two novels and several short stories earlier, when Ahab linked his own powers to those of the sun. The reason is not difficult to find. Ahab is part of a tradition of narrators in American literature whose power is defined in inverse relation to the power of others. His strength depends upon his ability to subdue the world outside himself and render it malleable to his own will. As he states at the end of "Sunset," "Over unsounded gorges, through the rifled hearts of mountains, under torrents' beds, unerringly I rush! Naught's an obstacle, naught's an angle to the iron way!" (Chap. 37).

Ahab describes himself according to the conventions of the mechanical sublime. He resembles a roaring locomotive, his iron will like iron tracks, converting nature into the setting for his own fixed purpose. Nature's death, then, has less to do with cities and commerce than with the purposes of the mind. Nature died the moment it was framed. It was murdered by a sublime and monomaniacal imagination.

Had Melville placed Ahab on the *deck* of the *Pequod,* rather than inside his cabin, the story might have been different. He would then resemble Ishmael, whose mast-head reveries suggest a direct and unmediated encounter with the landscape. Ishmael appears in many ways to be Ahab's foil. Where Ahab resembles Milton's Satan on Mount Niphates, "damned, most subtly and most malignantly! damned in the midst of Paradise," Ishmael is gifted "with the low, enjoying power" (Chap. 37). He is one with the crew — "my shout went up with theirs," – and he can sustain himself through the business of everyday life in a manner that eludes Ahab. If Ahab knows nature only as it is distanced and framed by sublime art, Ishmael exists as a figure in the landscape. He takes pleasure in the vagaries of fate, and would no more challenge the sun than miss out on a voyage to the ends of the world.

But Ishmael is a tricky character. He knows, as Ahab does not, how to live with ambiguity. Though he lacks Ahab's will to power, he shares Ahab's moments of visionary appetite. Above all, Ishmael possesses the same taste for things sublime that distinguishes Ahab. Only unlike Ahab, he can play with fire without getting burned. Ishmael does not need an iron will or an enclosing frame to control his vision. He plays instead with *words,* and can coax from the ambiguity of language worlds as bright and illuminating as Ahab's doomed sun. We learn from Ishmael not only how the sublime operates as a form of power, but how language functions to sublime ends.

And this is where Melville shares common ground with the artists whom he knew and admired. Both writers and painters were engaged in the creation of an American version of the sublime. If *Moby-Dick* is our national tale of questing, an account not just of boats and whales but of the imagination and its limits, then it also shares with the writings of Emerson and the landscapes of Cole and Durand an impulse toward the sublime. Whether in prose, poetry, or pigment, American art of the 1850s fermented with the energies of a visionary character it could barely contain.

When Is a Painting Most Like a Whale?

What began in eighteenth-century England as a taste for the wild and destructive concluded in mid-nineteenth-century America as a national way of seeing. And Melville was a part of that ferment.

1

Melville provides many warnings in *Moby-Dick,* some of them quite humorous, against a form of romantic revery associated with Emerson and his followers. In the chapter "The Mast-Head," Ishmael cautions an imaginary "young Platonist," more given to "unseasonable meditativeness" than to searching for whales, against standing watch on the perilous height of the mast-head. The problem involves more than a question of philosophy. It concerns the law of gravity and its untoward consequences for those who mistake the roll of the sea for the rhythms of their soul.

> But while this sleep, this dream is on ye, move your foot or hand an inch; slip your hold at all; and your identity comes back in horror. Over Descartian vortices you hover. And perhaps, at midday, in the fairest weather, with one half-throttled shriek you drop through that transparent air into the summer sea, no more to rise for ever. Heed it well, ye Pantheists! (Chap. 35)

Ishmael cautions the visionary pantheist, caught in an Emersonian moment of "midday," the "fairest weather," and "transparent air," not to mistake the pleasantries of nature for the realities of his own soul. The peril of such confusion is that the young philosopher risks, quite literally, losing his grip on reality and plunging, unwittingly, to the waiting seas below. Ishmael's warning represents more than an insight into the dangers of a particular strand of American thought. It is a good-natured form of self-admonishment, a caution against his own visionary penchants, and we do well to take Ishmael seriously on the matter. For the very confusion of nature and self that he warns against is precisely the stance he takes in the chapter.

Ishmael's notion of pantheism is a peculiarly romantic one: It emphasizes the *individual's* oneness with nature while playing down *God.* Ishmael's language is in fact closer to solipsism than pantheism, for the dangers he describes are those of a mind mis-

145

taking its own habits of thought for the workings of the world. Though the plight of Ishmael's pantheist begins properly enough with a dream of cosmic oneness, it soon takes its leave of the cosmos and slips unannounced into the realm of individual perception. The ocean becomes only a metaphor for the dreaming mind:

> lulled into such an opium-like listlessness of vacant, unconscious reverie is this absent-minded youth by the blending cadence of waves with thoughts, that at last he loses his identity; takes the mystic ocean at his feet for the visible image of that deep, blue, bottomless soul, pervading mankind and nature; *and* every strange, half-seen, gliding, beautiful thing that eludes him; every dimly-discovered, uprising fin of some undiscernible form, seems to him the embodiment of those elusive thoughts that only people the soul by continually flitting through it. (Chap. 35)

The key word here is "and," that apparently innocent conjunction that links the "bottomless soul, pervading mankind and nature" with those "elusive thoughts" flitting through the mind. What begins as a description of the dreaming self's unity with universal forces concludes, through the transition of Ishmael's "and," with a rewriting of nature as nothing more than a vast lexicon of the mind. The "and" does not continue but *contradicts* the thoughts that have preceded it. It reverses the emptying of self into nature that Ishmael initially describes, and substitutes for it a more malleable nature poured through the mold of human consciousness. Nature exists as nothing more than a vehicle for the individual's thoughts. Ishmael recovers himself in the next sentence. He returns to his original "enchanted mood," where the "spirit ebbs away to whence it came" and "becomes diffused through time and space." The solipsist is once again a pantheist.

But the rhetorical damage has been done. Under the guise of a continuity between self and nature – that sly little "and" – Ishmael has for a moment forgotten nature's vastness and reduced it to a metaphor, however undecipherable, for his own thoughts. What mystery there is to the sharky seas is bound now not by the globed rim of the horizon but by the circumference of the speaker's head. Like the pantheist he has just warned, Ishmael is guilty of a Cartesian split between mind and world. He has separated reality from

146

his thoughts just long enough to allow him to reduce reality – to reify it – to a sentiment of his own making. And the space in which he accomplishes this subordination of nature to mind is no greater than the word "and."

The irony of Ishmael's behavior here is that it resembles that of Emerson, the unnamed presence in the passage just quoted. Melville's attitude to Emerson is well known. He admired Emerson's visionary qualities at the same time as he despaired over Emerson's apparent inability to acknowledge evil.[2] Ishmael's "sunken-eyed young Platonist," glancing at the heavens while plunging into the seas below, parodies in cautionary fashion the plight of the budding transcendentalist. Melville presents us with an extreme version of Emersonian innocence, a state of mind that expands consciousness only by diminishing the material world and the dangers it contains. Ishmael's relation to Emerson, however, is more complicated than his tongue-in-cheek analogy suggests. For as we shall soon see, Ishmael shares far more with the bard of Concord than his comic caveat acknowledges.

2

Ishmael is not alone in his concern with Emersonian states of mind. Two years before the writing of *Moby-Dick*, Asher B. Durand had composed a Catskill wilderness scene in terms reminiscent of Emerson's *Nature*. Only Durand lacks Ishmael's teasing irony toward Emersonian conventions. *Kindred Spirits*, 1849 (Fig. 1), translates a moment of romantic epiphany – that instant when the veil of nature is lifted and the perceiver sees nature's hidden harmonies – into a spatial odyssey linking the foreground and background of his painting. Durand places the figures of Cole and Bryant on a stone outcropping at the center of the canvas. The rounded sweep of trees in the upper left half of the painting arches across the top and then bends down to the right, where it meets the answering line of cliffs. The movement of trees and cliffs creates a circular frame within the larger rectangle of the canvas itself. This circular space opens at its center – like the pupil of a cosmic eyeball – into the visionary depth of the background, a movement

Figure 1. Asher B. Durand, *Kindred Spirits*, 1849. (New York: New York Public Library)

reinforced by an abundance of angular foreground objects that point, like vectors, toward the light of sky and clouds in the distance.

This motion from foreground to background is summarized in the figure of a broken tree trunk lying in the ravine beneath the central promontory. The right half of the tree plunges downward

148

to the earth, anchoring the viewer in the painting's foreground; its left portion points to the ribbon of water and light that conducts the eye into the background. The tree thus summarizes, through its divided form, the tension in the painting between surface image and recessional movement back into space. It adumbrates the larger odyssey of the viewer through the painting at the same time as it achieves its own visual repair: It directs the spectator away from the death that it hints at to the distant promise of the background sky.[3]

The drama of the painting lies in the transformation of a circular foreground into a zigzag recession: The viewer must break out of the luxuriant foreground world, where individual leaves and twigs define nature precisely, in order to ascend along a pathway marked by streams and soaring birds to a more generalized world of light and energy. Or, to take our cue from the foreground log, the immersion in the world of nature and natural process in the foreground leads only to death without a corresponding movement into the background through (and perhaps beyond) nature to the truths — those values and spiritual laws — that nature incarnates. *Kindred Spirits* thus defines through its visual structure a moment of epiphany central to the Emersonian world view. Transcendence for Durand, as for the tradition of landscape writing and painting he represents, entails a twofold dialectic: an embrace of the natural world in all its particularity (enforced visually by the circular structure of the foreground) and a moment of release when the natural is refigured as the spiritual and foreground yields to background. The "kindred spirits" of the title thus refers not simply to the "sister arts" represented by the painter and poet on the ledge, or even, at a further remove, to the larger drama of the individual in nature, but to the ultimate possibility of unity itself: to a chain of being so constituted that the natural yields forever to the spiritual, the invocation of the former inexorably summoning the presence of the latter.

But that is precisely what Ishmael warns against in "The Mast-Head": a world where unity is so facile an achievement that the eye forgets the perils to which the body is subjected. Notice the way in which Durand removes from the painting any real threat of bodily harm. Though he stations his figures on a promontory, and thus subjects them to the sort of potential vertigo that afflicts Ishmael's dreaming Platonist, Durand, unlike Ishmael, proceeds to *domesticate* his space into a womblike enclosure that protects rather than threatens its figures. He renders motion back into space an affair of the eye rather than a threat to the body. As the gesture of the foreground painter suggests, one can do no more than *point* to the background epiphany. Our voyage back beyond the picture plane is thus an adventure of the mind rather than an entrance into a physically accessible, or even permissible, space. We proceed skyward according to the imperatives of consciousness. Durand thus creates a world in which nature exists as an echo of the thinking self, and regeneration (that influx of power symbolized by the bird soaring toward the viewer) occurs as a form of perception.

Durand's epiphanic landscape provides the perfect foil for Ishmael's satirical vision. With a Catskill outcropping for his masthead, with a wilderness scene for his "unshored" ocean (and with very little irony), Durand constructs a state where the "spirit ebbs away" and "becomes diffused through time and space." His celebratory image of the individual's at-homeness in the landscape represents the type of shortsighted optimism that Ishmael so gaily demolishes. What Ishmael cannot forget, as Durand's figures easily do, are the steep heights and precipitous depths over which they stand.

And yet – and this is the key question – does Durand's epiphantic vision illustrate Emerson's philosophy as closely as our analogy suggests? The Emerson present in Durand's spiritualized space, the vatic Emerson whom Ishmael so keenly parodies, is nowhere present in his own writings. He is rather a straw figure, an easy setup, abstracted and reduced from his own work. When we actually turn to a page of *Nature*, Emerson's first book and earliest transcendentalist manifesto, we find not a promiscuous lover of nature ready to romance the first tree he encounters, but a complicated singer of the self. He is more a solipsist than a pantheist, and in this regard he is a closer, and perhaps stranger, bedfellow to Ishmael than Melville might want to acknowledge. And that, of course, is where the story gets interesting.

3

In a remarkable paragraph in the opening pages of *Nature,* Emerson undergoes a spiritual odyssey not unlike the transformation that undergirds the experience of *Kindred Spirits.* The crucial difference, however (other than the obvious one that Emerson's account pre-dates Durand's image by more than a decade and might well have served as a model for the later experience), lies in the role that nature plays for each figure. It is everywhere present in Durand and almost nowhere in Emerson. This is a rather daunting assertion to make about an author whose major book is titled *Nature* and whose reputation is based on a love of things out-of-doors. But Emerson was a clever man and a brilliant writer, and his uses of "nature" were anything but natural.

The famous "transparent eyeball" passage of *Nature* commences, as previous commentators have noted, not in the countryside but on the Boston Commons:

> Crossing a bare common, in snow puddles, at twilight, under a clouded sky, without having in my thoughts any occurrence of special good fortune, I have enjoyed a perfect exhilaration. I am glad to the brink of fear. In the woods, too, a man casts off his years, as the snake his slough, and at what period soever of life is always a child. In the woods is perpetual youth. . . . In the woods, we return to reason and faith. There I feel that nothing can befall me in life, – no disgrace, no calamity (leaving me my eyes), which nature cannot repair. Standing on the bare ground, – my head bathed by the blithe air and uplifted into infinite space, – all mean egotism vanishes. I become a transparent eyeball; I am nothing; I see all; the currents of the Universal Being circulate through me; I am part and parcel of God. . . . In the wilderness, I find something more dear and connate than in streets or villages. In the tranquil landscape, and especially in the distant line of the horizon, man beholds somewhat as beautiful as his own nature.[4]

The key to this passage can be found in its opening lines, and especially in the manner in which Emerson situates himself in space. The passage begins in a state of transition: The speaker is in the process of "Crossing a bare common." He is already in motion when we first observe him, and his movements carry with them the suggestion of a moral geography. To cross a bare common is not only to initiate a process of change, a pilgrim's progress, but to fill the emptiness of the common with significance: to cross it, to place it under the sign of the cross. Both "crossing" and "common" are puns. The former has religious overtones, whereas the latter suggests a vernacular world, the common realm of everyday experience. "Crossing a bare common," then, is not only an act of secular faith, an investment of the vernacular with significance, but also a negating of the everyday, a crossing out of the ordinary in the name of that which is to follow, the extraordinary. This second meaning of "crossing," an allusion not just to theology but to the negation, the emptying out that must precede salvation, is reinforced by the description of the common as "bare." It has been denuded, emptied of its color by the "clouded" "twilight" hour of the day, and shorn of its relation both to nature (it is no longer a wilderness, but the heart of a city) and to society (where are the people?).

We encounter the term "bare" again several lines later in the description that immediately precedes the "transparent eyeball" experience. "Standing on the bare ground, – my head bathed by the blithe air and uplifted into infinite space, – all mean egotism vanishes." The "bare common" has become the "bare ground" here. It is both more anonymous than in the previous description and, for that very reason, more central to the experience that follows. The bare ground exists as a precondition, rhetorically and metaphysically, for the "uplifted" head. The act of vision depends upon a previous moment of negation. Before the speaker can *see*, before he can "dilate and conspire" with the universe around him, he must first reduce its otherness to a manageable form. And that happens as early as his initial "crossing" of the common.

What we learn from the earlier episode – what the later description confirms – is a process of displacement in which the speaker situates himself at an ever greater remove from nature. To cross a bare common is to cross out nature, to eradicate it as a scene of anything but the author's own vision. When two lines later we enter the woods at last, we arrive by force of analogy: "In the woods, too, a man casts off his years, as the snake his slough, and at what period soever of life is always a child." The transition from bare commons to the woods is effected by the word "too": "In the woods, too . . ." The "too" tells us that we have moved in analogous fashion from the commons to the woods, that in the woods *as on* the commons, a certain experience of divestiture occurs. "Too" then functions as a hidden simile. It reminds us that we move from one location to another only imaginatively, *as if* the commons were the woods, *as if* we were there. We learn that crossing any bare commons, when it is an act significantly done, requires motion no greater than a metaphor, and nature is simply that which is emptied out, erased, crossed over.

Childhood, then, is the endpoint of a twofold experience: the emptying out of the old, like a snake shedding his slough, and the creation in its stead of an imaginative self empowered by its own rhetoric. Childhood is rhetoric rightly learned, the capacity of tropes and language to fill nature's vacuum. It is little wonder that Emerson should subsequently find himself a transparent eyeball. It is a trope that not only combines in oxymoronic fashion the visual and cerebral (like trying to imagine what thought *looks like*) but defines visionary experience as a form of self-aggrandizement. The loss of "all mean egotism" requires more than a mystical congruence of self and world. True power occurs only in a moment of *representation* when vision and language are conjoined and the self is at its "ocular" best ("I *see* all"). The ego is not so much dissolved as concentrated in a state of heightened awareness, its perceptual possibilities intensified rather than transcended (why else be a transparent *eyeball*?). What Emerson provides us with, then, is not a metalinguistic event, an experience of union with nature outside language and time, but a moment of epiphany informed by the possibilities of perception.

That, I take it, is the force of Emerson's perceptual pilgrimage. Nature is fitted to the mind's shape, it circulates through us, and our own powers of seeing come to substitute for the common void of reality. The dualistic rhythms of Emerson's prose — "I am nothing; I see all," — simply repeat the pattern of negation and plentitude supplied by the opening passage. And *what*, we may ask after all this, do we actually *see*? Why, ourselves, of course. Emerson concludes his experience of power and vision with a line as sweet and smooth as country butter: "In the tranquil landscape, and especially in the distant line of the horizon, man beholds somewhat as beautiful as his own nature." The allusion to the "line of the horizon" is meant to suggest an image of expansion that defines the self's rather than the world's boundaries. For as Emerson tells us at the conclusion of his sentence, "man beholds somewhat as beautiful as his own nature." Nature has become "his own nature," not just a possession of the visionary self (*"his* own nature"), but a version of himself: It is his *own* nature that we behold. The experience of the transparent eyeball has become a study in self-portraiture. The story behind the story is how one comes to possess nature as a version of oneself.

And this returns us to Ishmael and his young Platonist. What Ishmael shares with Emerson – what Durand lacks – is a rapaciousness of vision that swallows reality whole and converts it into a version of the self. The dreamy-eyed Platonist, you will recall, was doing the opposite: He was flowing with the ocean of life in mystical oneness. Or at least that is what he *thought* he was doing. Not until Ishmael's sly little "and" turned him into a closet Emersonian, a hidden solipsist, did we begin to understand the game that Ishmael was playing. In the guise of warning us against pantheistic reveries, he was actually steering us away from the *real* danger: a form of visual and intellectual self-aggrandizement that reduces reality to a cipher at the same time as it renders man the cipher maker. The Emerson Ishmael implicitly satirizes exists nowhere but in Ishmael's text. He is a vacant-eyed worshipper of nature. But the real Emerson, the dangerous because sublime Emerson, is the true subject of Ishmael's concern. And that Emerson, *our* Emerson, exists not in Ishmael's satire but in his rhetorical doings, his metaphoric comings and goings. What Ishmael is not telling us is that he is our most Emersonian of narrators.

4

There is another way to define Ishmael's relation to Emerson, and that is to say that each represents an American version of the sublime. This is not the sublime of Burke and his eighteenth-century followers, who preached a power in nature, and a corresponding faculty of appreciation in man, that overwhelmed all of

154

our usual notions of order. Burke's sublime was a transgressive one: It viewed nature as a punishing father and then transformed that punishment into a spectacle that could be safely viewed – and enjoyed – from a distance. By the time of Melville in the mid-nineteenth century, the sublime had undergone radical surgery. The presiding "physician" had been Immanuel Kant, the philosopher from Koenigsberg, who grafted large portions of Burke's sublime from nature as an external power to the *observer* within nature. The result was a new emphasis on perception itself. To behold the sublime in nature was not simply to witness the elements in all their grandeur but to appropriate that grandeur as a *metaphor* for consciousness. The question was no longer when is a landscape most like a father (and an angry one at that), but how is the horizon only another version of thought, a boundary to consciousness?

Kant's ideas underwent many transformations in the early nineteenth century. They surfaced in altered form in the writings of the English romantics and appeared, ghostlike, to haunt the literary corpus of Samuel Taylor Coleridge. Where they took deepest root, however, was in America, and here they grew at a prodigious pace, breathed to life in the writings of Emerson and nurtured by a certain cultural imperialism that was always happy to convert, in Emerson's terms, the NOT ME into the ME.

For that is what the sublime in the nineteenth century meant: an astonishing capacity of mind, an ability to consume the world as nothing more than a plenum of nutrients in that characteristically American project of self-making. At its most audacious, the sublime entailed a virtual substitution of self for world; it was an egotistical affair conceived in pride and consummated in an incestuous twining of nature back into the self, the NOT ME into the ME. The key to this project was language, the uncanny talent of words to usurp the place of things and to define possession as only another manner of speaking. As Thoreau, another of Emerson's disciples, wrote of his relation to the Yankee farmer on a neighboring farm, "I took his word for his deed, for I dearly loved to talk." The sublime artist deeded himself primogeniture over all the world, for it was his to inherit at a price no greater than words. The strategy was as brilliant as it was simple. Convert nature into language: Render that which is other, prior to, or outside the self into a version accessible to the self and you shall reign as a (figurative) monarch over all you see.

To understand the peculiarly *linguistic* quality of sublime art in America, we need to return again to the world of painting. For it is here, where we might least expect to find it, that we encounter one of the earliest conjunctions of language with sublime vision. Nine years before Emerson published *Nature*, Thomas Cole created a painting that we know today as *Landscape Composition, St. John in the Wilderness*, 1827 (Fig. 2). The canvas shows John the Baptist exhorting a group of followers in the midst of a craggy mountain setting. The tiny human figures stand on a jutting rock outcropping that is itself suspended precipitously over a deep ravine. In the upper center of the canvas an enormous stone pinnacle surges skyward. The canvas divides into foreground and middle-ground planes (Fig. 3). The figures and outcropping in the foreground call up feelings of vertigo: Whatever stability the rock may offer is counterbalanced by its pendulous position in space. At any moment, the foreground world with its tiny human denizens may simply collapse into the void. The middle-ground pinnacle, to the contrary, stands barren and without signs of habitation; it seems massive, weighted, and inhuman in comparison with the foreground world. This contrast in scale between foreground and middle ground, between precarious human event and elemental natural setting, adds a certain elegiac tone to the painting. The mountain will survive long after the humans have disappeared.

Or so we might initially believe. A closer examination of the foreground reveals a story significantly different from whatever conclusions we might draw upon a first viewing. St. John stands silhouetted against the canyon wall opposite him. A plain wooden cross at his side echoes in its simplicity the Baptist's cruciform gestures. Both cross and Baptist seem equally vulnerable when compared to the heedless authority of rock and stone. The two slender sticks of the cross can scarcely compete with the vertical thrust of the pinnacle against which they are set, and the frail figure of the Baptist seems no more than a foil for the inhuman power of the landscape. Were we to end our description here, we

Figure 2. Thomas Cole, *Landscape Composition, St. John in the Wilderness,* 1827. (Hartford, Conn.: Wadsworth Atheneum)

would have to conclude that the human figures play only a marginal role in the larger composition.

And yet there is more within the painting than initially meets the eye. To perceive what significance lurks here, we need to turn to the gnarled trees that straddle the foreground promontory at the

Figure 3. *Landscape Composition, St. John in the Wilderness,* detail, figure of St. John.

extreme right. These trees adumbrate through their shapes the presence of the cross. Like it, they are elemental in form and juxtaposed visually to the valley wall. What distinguishes trees from cross, however, is the symbolic role played only by the latter. The trees possess no semiotic significance; they remain natural objects in a mute world. Cole's trees display no intrinsic meaning until they are marshaled in the service of a symbolic system. Wood remains wood until its rearrangement serves larger linguistic ends, until it becomes a *cross,* a sign in a larger signifying system, at which point it is suddenly transformed from two sticks, nature merely, into an instance of symbol making. Through language, nature is rendered the servant of forces larger than itself.

And that is the heart of Cole's sublime, the key to the drama represented by St. John the Baptist and his followers. Nature is "crossed out" for Cole, as it will later be for Emerson; its power is voided or negated and transferred from the landscape to the human figures who occupy it. What we learn from the cross is that the forces of nature, which once threatened the individual, are now themselves subject to a new order. By a gesture as simple and complex as placing two sticks together, the objects of the land-scape become vehicles of human expression. They cease to func-tion as elements of the landscape and operate instead as signs within a signifying system.

What happens in Cole's sublime, as in Emerson's, is a reversal of power made possible by an act of language, literalized here in the image of the cross. The cross summarizes within itself the relation of vehicle to tenor that governs all metaphors: It is an object that points beyond itself to meanings that it more or less arbitrarily represents. The cross is a vehicle, a symbolic instrument, and in the context of Cole's painting it carries a twofold meaning: The-ologically it points to the passion and resurrection of Christ, and linguistically it incarnates the capacity to signify that is the hall-mark of all language.

And that is where the sublime comes in. The sublime may be defined as a form of conversion. It transforms the otherness of the landscape – the threat it poses to the human figures as an alien terrain – into the material of vision. And it does so through lan-guage, by rendering nature the stuff of metaphor. If Cole's St. John were defined by a sense of humor rather than a sense of religion, he would be very close to Melville's Ishmael. Both figures, in their more sublime moments, view the world from great heights, whence each proceeds to transform the threat presented by nature into an opportunity for self-expression. They both render nature's powers a trope for their own. And this "troping" through nature, whether expressed in the imagery of religion or whaling voyages, is what the sublime is all about in mid-nineteenth-century America.

5

Ishmael's story represents a test of the proposition that the world may be brought under the sway of language. His relation to events around him depends upon his use of words. In "Cetology," we catch Ishmael at his favorite labor: transforming his observations and arcane learning into a form of word play. He tells us at the outset:

> It is some systematized exhibition of the whale in his broad genera, that I would now fain put before you. Yet is it no easy task. The classification of the constituents of a chaos, nothing less is here essayed. (Chap. 32)

The term "essayed" alerts us to the design of Ishmael's project. He will not only attempt (essay) to comprehend the whale, but he will do so as a literary exercise (essay). Ishmael commences his cetological observations with a bow toward objectivity. He hurls every scrap of knowledge available to him at the unnamed significance of the whale, hoping to overcome nature's silence by the force of his learning. "Cetology" thus begins with what might be termed a "shotgun" approach to whaling: Ishmael loads his metaphoric gun with the fodder of human knowledge, takes aim at whales in particular and the universe in general, and then gently lets go. For the next several pages, we see scattered over the text the debris of human knowledge mingled with fragments of whale.

On the whole, it is a rather messy approach. Ishmael later admits that "As yet . . . the sperm whale, scientific or poetic, lives not complete in any literature. Far above all other hunted whales, his is an unwritten life." The effort to capture the whale within the hunt of knowledge is a failure. Ishmael accordingly rejects the classifications of Linnaeus and modern science and asserts, on the advice of some of his old sea friends and the biblical book of *Jonah*, that "a whale is a spouting fish with a horizontal tail. There you have him." He abandons science altogether and substitutes for natural history the Gospel of Whales according to Ishmael.

What follows is a transformation of whales into books grouped according to printers' conventions. In language redolent of biblical rhetoric and epic formula, Ishmael proclaims "the grand divisions of the entire whale host."

> First: According to magnitude I divide the whales into three primary BOOKS (subdivisible into CHAPTERS), and these shall comprehend them all, both small and large.
> I. THE FOLIO WHALE; II. the OCTAVO WHALE; III. the DUODECIMO WHALE. (Chap. 32)

Ishmael's strategy here is to replace learning with laughter — not *any* laughter, but his own deconstructive version of laughing. His undercuts the myth of objective knowledge with which he began and playfully proceeds to textualize his world, measuring reality according to the dimensions of books. His conversion of leviathans into folio sizes shifts the focus of "Cetology" from whales (what we thought Ishmael was talking about) to language (what in fact the chapter is about). In the process, Ishmael domesticates what is foreign in nature into a version of the familiar.

But it is only a version. Whales, of course, are not the same as books, and that is Ishmael's point. The *tone* of Ishmael's language — his tongue-in-cheek humor — alerts us to the fact that Ishmael's efforts are only in jest. We laugh when we read "Cetology" because we are dealing with a game of cosmic proportions, for Ishmael, unlike Einstein's God, willingly plays dice with the universe. What we learn from Ishmael's mock-heroic language is that the imagination depends upon one condition in its dealings with the world: It must acknowledge the fictionality of its own efforts. Ishmael's humor alerts us to the *as if* procedures of the imagination. We must act *as if* whales were texts, for only by subjecting nature to language do we render it significant. Meaning, then, is not something we find but something we *bring* to nature, and, lest we forget our contribution and mistake our efforts for those of the cosmos, humor is what reminds us that meaning is only a game that language plays. Ishmael's transmogrification of mammals into books, a task at once humorous and loving, is his way of insisting that whales be bearers of meaning, even if that meaning is nothing more than the fictionality of all meaning.

Of course, Ishmael is not always so loquacious. When he first encounters Queequeg in the book's opening chapters, he finds himself speechless. In a scene full of comic happenstance, the most curious incident of all is Ishmael's momentary loss of language. Ishmael, as you will recall, has been sitting in bed, watching with amazement the rituals of a bald-headed stranger who is unaware of his presence. With growing horror, Ishmael realizes that the figure he is gazing at behaves suspiciously like a South Seas savage. "Had not the stranger stood between me and the door, I would have bolted out of it quicker than ever I bolted a dinner."

Ishmael doesn't bolt. What he does instead is observe, a comic witness to Queequeg's inscrutable rituals. The bolting, when it comes, is entirely Queequeg's. He grabs his tomahawk, puffs out "great clouds of tobacco smoke" and leaps into bed, unaware that Ishmael is anything more than an unruly fold of the sheets.

And that is where the curiosity lies. Ishmael is invisible to Queequeg; when Ishmael wants to talk, he can't. Realizing that Queequeg is about to leap into bed, Ishmael decides that it is time to announce his presence. "I thought it was high time, now or never, before the light was put out, to break the spell in which I had so long been bound." But he misses his chance. Queequeg pounces into bed while Ishmael is still deliberating what to do.

> But the interval I spent in deliberating what to say, was a fatal one. . . . The next moment the light was extinguished, and this wild cannibal, tomahawk between his teeth, sprang into bed with me. I sang out, I could not help it now; and giving a sudden grunt of astonishment he began feeling me. (Chap. 3)

Ishmael's response to this heathen invasion is as inarticulate as Queequeg's "sudden grunt."

> Stammering out something, I know not what, I rolled away from him against the wall, and then conjured him, whoever or whatever he might be, to keep quiet, and let me get up and light the lamp again. But his guttural responses satisfied me at once that he but ill comprehended my meaning. (Chap. 3).

Ishmael's invisibility at this point is tied to his momentary lack of language. He cannot be seen by Queequeg because he has no voice. His silence before Queequeg's leap into bed robs him of any opportunity to assert his presence or retain even modest control over a situation where bad yields quickly to worse.

Were we to diagram Ishmael's story, we might divide it into parts labeled "before" and "after." *Before* Queequeg's great leap forward, Ishmael is a mock-visionary self alone in the bed; *after* Queequeg jumps into the bed, Ishmael is an awkward body, subject both to Queequeg's surprise and to his unintended advances ("he began feeling me"). What separates the two is language. Language is what allows Ishmael to retain his visionary status, or, to be more precise, it is the *lapse* of language that subjects Ishmael to Queequeg's bodily interrogation. Language is what defends the visionary self, however comically presented, against its own bodily status.

We have seen this situation before in *Moby-Dick,* or rather, in the context of the book's chronology, we will see it again. In "The Mast-Head," Ishmael relies upon language — his own visionary powers — not only to dilate with the universe but to protect himself against the consequences of too bodily a response to gravity. "The Mast-Head" represents a rewriting of Ishmael's initial encounter with Queequeg; it is the same tale with a different ending. In both, the focus is upon visionary action, whether set comically in a dark bed at night or, more plausibly, on the mast-head of a whaling vessel. And in both, the moment of vision yields to its attendant dangers. In "The Spouter-Inn," Queequeg represents as real a bodily threat to the discumbobulated Ishmael as the ocean depths do to the bleary-eyed Platonist. What distinguishes the two chapters is the nature of the threat presented and the manner in which it is resolved. And here the chapters work antithetically: What appears to threaten Ishmael with bodily harm in "The Spouter-Inn" proves to be a boon instead. Queequeg becomes Ishmael's closest friend and alter ego. In "The Mast-Head," to the contrary, what appears benign and inviting — the blue of the sky and ocean — leads to the possibility of death, that unsanctified plunge to the ocean floor.

What do we learn from all this? That Ishmael's encounter with Queequeg, like the "mystick's" oceanic feelings, are studies in the limits of consciousness. Each episode carries us from a visionary state to a moment of bodily threat, and when we arrive there, when we find ourselves at the margins of thought and language, we are confronted with two alternatives. We may, like the young Platonist, ignore the limits before us and plunge headlong into the sea (did you ever see a Platonist dive *feet* first?). Or, like Ishmael with Queequeg, we may discover in the very lapse of language the possibility of new experiences. The real threat, in effect, comes not from language but from ourselves: It lies in our inability to discriminate limits, to recognize where our discourse ends and someone else's begins. What we learn from Ishmael is not to take our own vision too exclusively. We need to make our peace with the *lapses*. For that is where Queequeg dwells.

What does all this have to do with the sublime? A great deal, for Ishmael's story represents an egotistical sublime continually testing its own limits. Ishmael is surrounded by things that go bump in the night, a world that repeatedly asserts its otherness to him. Whether that otherness takes the form of a South Seas savage, a wounded captain, a hunted whale, or an inscrutable universe, it is always there. Ishmael's response, in turn, is consistent. He affirms the very lapses that hem in a figure like Ahab — lapses that define the boundaries of his own discourse. When Ishmael speaks, two things happen. Whatever he touches turns to language (Ishmael as sublime narrator), and whatever he touches touches him back (the sublime discovering its limits). The first of these two moments represents Ishmael's effort to convert the world into a version of himself, whereas the second characterizes those instances of rupture in the text when we lose Ishmael's voice altogether. The question is: How do we reconcile the idea of the sublime with the idea of limits — don't the two represent a contradiction in terms? Or, in terms of Ishmael's story, what do we learn about the sublime from Ishmael's silences?

6

To answer our questions, we return once more to mid-nineteenth-century American painting. We have been dealing with the sublime thus far as an egotistical event that operates through the medium of language. We haven't considered, however, the prices language exacts for its services. Language was not a neutral medium for Melville and his contemporaries. It came with certain tendencies and imperatives of its own. To understand Ishmael, we need to know not only how he converts the real into a form of language game, but what rules the game imposes upon its players. And nowhere is the tension between the sublime as an egotistical affair and the sublime as a form of language more evident than in the landscapes of Frederic E. Church. Church was a student of

Thomas Cole. His landscapes of the 1850s commanded prices higher than those previously paid for any American painting. Church's flair for melodrama together with his tendency to paint exotic scenery made him the most prominent figure in the second generation of Hudson River school painters. His art provides us with a chronicle of the sublime as it negotiates its own contradictory imperatives. We discover in his canvases both the evasions and the affirmations that undergird a narrative like Ishmael's.

In *The Andes of Ecuador* of 1855 (Fig. 4), Church provides the viewer with an allegory of American national destiny. Church harnesses the traditions of the sublime for New World purposes. He renders a local, if idealized, landscape into an almost religious vision of birth and resurrection (a way of seeing that Church shared with many of his contemporaries). The painting effects its transformation of secular into sacred by two means: iconographically, though its juxtaposition of earthly crosses in the lower left of the canvas with the heavenly cross of light in the center, and in more painterly fashion through its use of light. The sun presides over a world in which matter is converted into energy and each day begins with the promise of new creation.

Figure 4. Frederic E. Church, *The Andes of Ecuador*, 1855. (Winston-Salem, N.C.: Reynolda House Museum of American Art)

Figure 5. Frederic E. Church, signature, letter to Mr. Warren, May 23, 1856. (Philadelphia: The Historical Society of Pennsylvania)

Church loved to pun: He occasionally signed letters with a picture of a church (Fig. 5). If we look closely at *The Andes of Ecuador*, we find not only a church or monastery nestled in the foreground hills to the left of center, but also a recurrent series of light-filled crosses emanating downward along a vertical axis that literally inscribes the painter (or his iconic surrogate, the cross) into the landscape. We need not avail ourselves of the pun to appreciate the way in which the painter places *himself* at the center of his canvas. The painting subjugates matter to the laws of light and allows no refuge from its spellbinding energy. It celebrates in sublime fashion the powers of consciousness over the natural world, a world where light almost literally dematerializes the landscape that reflects it.

Church subordinates nature to the monopoly of mind in two ways: graphically, through the unifying efforts of color, tone, and composition; and verbally or iconically, through those puns that place the painter at the heart of his world. The canvas is composed of a series of concentric circles (or semicircles) around the organizing presence of the sun. This drive toward unity is counterpointed by a progression of rectangular planes, which in their movement from foreground to middle ground transform the landscape visually into a sequence of steps culminating in altarlike fashion before the regal and enthroned sun. To move from foreground to background is to undergo a progressive spiritualization, a dematerialization, that dissolves matter into light and renders all nature subject to the laws of the sun. Church's cross of light not only crosses out nature as anything more than a reflection of itself but proceeds, in Emersonian fashion, to fill the vacuum left through nature's negation with its own image. The impression of unity is reinforced by the monochromatic palette and muted colors that bind together Church's world.

But there is a problem, perhaps we might even say a *repression*, afoot, and we do well to note it. A deep chasm runs from the right foreground to the lower center of the painting, where it intersects with the vertical axis of Church's cross of light. This chasm announces, or at least suggests, a bifurcation of reality larger than the artist's monism would allow. The foreground breach in the landscape reminds us that Church is attempting to repair by color what has been sundered by composition, and that the covert drama of the painting so intent upon its own monistic unity concerns that hidden but lingering hint of dualism present in the canvas's foreground.

A brief bit of detective work brings us to Church's teacher,

Figure 6. Thomas Cole, *Expulsion from the Garden of Eden*, 1827. (Boston: Museum of Fine Arts)

Thomas Cole, who had painted three decades earlier *Expulsion from the Garden of Eden*, 1827 (Fig. 6). Note in both paintings an angled chasm that divides the foreground into separate realms, a mated pair of palm trees framing the composition on the left, and a sloping series of waterways that eventuate on the right in a quiet lake whose water plunges into the chasm. *The Andes of Ecuador* not only alludes to Cole through its deployment of a foreground space adapted from the *Expulsion* but proceeds to rewrite – or repaint – Cole in two ways: first by naturalizing Cole's more allegorical landscape, and then by replacing Cole's chiaroscuro and dualism with its own monochromatic unity. The painting moves from a bifurcated Colean foreground to a dazzling vision of unity in the background.

What we witness in these images of birth and creation (Church) and the fall and expulsion (Cole) are alternative accounts of the sublime. To appreciate Church's painting, we must understand the contrast it invokes between Cole's radically divided landscape and

Church's all-encompassing monism, his ability to restore that Edenic light in the right *half* of Cole's painting to the *whole* of his canvas. By rendering Cole a painter of dualisms and identifying himself, through the sun and cross in the sky, with the powers of a lost Eden, Church creates an image of Paradise regained. Church's painting provides an answer to Cole's *Expulsion:* It restores the light of Eden to the whole of the canvas. It is as if the pupil has not only memorialized the master (note again the shrinelike setting of the left foreground cross) but substitued for the latter's vision an image of self-repair and ultimately self-origination that claims for itself the sole power of creation. There is nothing in Church's sky to compete with his sun. He presides self-sufficient over his own light-infused world.

Or to phrase the matter alternatively, Church creates here an image of the egotistical sublime. He converts the past (Cole's *Expulsion*) into a version of himself at the same time as he renders nature as a metaphor for consciousness in general and the artist in particular. What begins publicly as a study of national destiny concludes privately as a portrait of the artist as a young man. Church thus resembles Ishmael (and, behind him, Emerson). For each figure, vision is always a two-step affair: an act of negation followed by a rewriting of the negated as a version of oneself, an absorption of nature into the language of the self.

Several years later, however, in *Cotopaxi,* 1862 (Fig. 7), Church returns to his relation with Cole from an altered perspective. His composition is now divided into dual realms in a manner reminiscent of Cole's *Expulsion.* The X-shaped or chiastic structure of the landscape denies the viewer the security of the fixed-point perspective that characterized *The Andes of Ecuador* and requires instead that we reverse our original orientation to the painting in moving from the foreground cliffs to the volcano or sun diagonally opposite in the background. The sky, like the land, is divided and uncentered; volcano and sun serve as dual foci for an unstated parabola.

Cotopaxi marks a turning point in Church's conception of the egotistical sublime. If we understand Church's volcano to echo Cole's own use of volcanic imagery, then *Cotopaxi,* in both its

Figure 7. Frederic E. Church, *Cotopaxi*, 1862. (Reading, Pa.: Reading Public Museum and Art Gallery)

iconography and its chiastic composition, represents a belated recognition of Church's indebtedness to Cole. *Cotopaxi* acknowledges what *The Andes of Ecuador* had attempted to suppress: the knowledge that all art is born from the traces of past art. The sublime, then, is an intertextual affair, conceived, if not in sin, then at least in its painterly equivalent, a world crowded with past images that permits no more than redactions, reinterpretations, of itself.

We know this in *Cotopaxi* because of the relation of sun to volcano. The two are united by a plume of dark smoke that forms, in its arc around the sun, the upper lid of an eyeball. The lower lid is defined by the curved line of the horizon. This is not Emerson's transparent eyeball but a bloody and apocalyptic organ, locked into a world it must share with others and dependent for its very definition upon a peak set to its side. To see is to *share* in this canvas, to construct a world distinguished not by its promise of newness, as in *The Andes of Ecuador*, but by its entanglement with the residue and debris of the past: that serpentine trail of volcanic smoke. In the fiery relation of volcano to sun, Colean trope to Churchian icon, we encounter an allegory of indebtedness that

170

belies the myth of originality. *Cotopaxi* thus demythologizes what the *The Andes of Ecuador* held to be central: that image of a new day, a new creation, untarnished by ties to the past. *Cotopaxi* thematizes instead, through its dual foci and chiastic construction, its own intertextual indebtedness. Without revision, the painting tells us, there is no vision.

And this returns us to Ishmael, whose narrative lapses resemble those moments of suppression in Church's canvases. What we learn from each is that language is a haunted medium: It comes with its own echoes and conventions. The ghost in Church's art is Cole. His compositions echo throughout Church's work, belying the very possibility of a sublime so egotistical that it can be sustained by nothing beyond itself. Queequeg similarly is Ishmael's spook (one of many), a figure of foreignness who intrudes upon Ishmael's comic narration. Queequeg, we should remember, is not only a person but a living system of representation. His most salient characteristic — the thing Ishmael notices about him first — is the network of hieroglyphic markings that cover his body. These markings return us to the linguistic dimension undergirding his relation to Ishmael; they are reminders that the sublime entails more than thought in confrontation with its bodily limits. The sublime is also an action of texts upon past texts. Ishmael's genius lies in his ability to read Queequeg, not as a specific text, for he can never fully decode Queequeg, but as a *prior* text. What Ishmael recognizes in Queequeg is a system of language different from his own. Ishmael's moments of silence, then, are like suture points in his narrative where other texts, other voices, make their presence felt. Ishmael's ability to bed down with Queequeg, whom he will later decide "was on the whole a clean, comely looking cannibal," represents a recuperation of the sublime in the face of its own limits.

Those limits, in turn, are imposed by the very otherness of language, its refusal of originality as anything more than an act of quotation. The egotistical sublime, from this point of view, is a clever act composed of equal amounts of quotation (for that is all language allows) and the suppression of one's sources (for that is what self-origination requires). What we learn from Ishmael, as from Church, is the capacity of the sublime both to affirm and to evade its boundaries by recognizing its own textual status. The sublime, then, is more than an egotistical event. It is an act of language predicated upon a recognition of otherness: an understanding that all writing, like all reading, stems from other and prior texts.

The dilemma of the sublime, then, lies in its need to balance two contradictory claims. On the one hand, it crosses out all of that which is other in order to re-create it in its own image; on the other hand, it harbors within itself, like an ill-digested meal, traces of past texts that refuse to be assimilated. Queequeg is one such text for Ishmael, as Cole was for Church. Queequeg represents the mystery of language itself, and Sphinx-like, he will not be answered. Yet it is not Queequeg who is to be feared in *Moby-Dick;* his cannibalism is relatively benign. It is Ishmael who is the book's ultimate cannibal, for what he devours are words, sentences, and paragraphs: whole systems of representation. And the reason he survives, the reason we love him, is that he doesn't care what he eats. The chewing is all.

Ishmael's endless capacity of incorporation, his ability to find nourishment from the most unlikely sources, sustains him throughout *Moby-Dick.* He is a cannibal of all texts, all experiences, a Zarathustrian joymaker for whom the pleasure of the game far exceeds all issues of gain or loss. His ability to garner life from the most unlikely sources, to buoy himself up at the novel's conclusion upon Queequeg's mystically inscribed coffin, renders him a figure of the fullest intertextuality, at once original and derived. His identity is both centered and dispersed, held together by the centripetal pull of the sublime toward an egotistical center and dissolved again by the centrifugal tendency of language to unravel into a cacophany of foreign voices. He thus embodies that tension within the romantic sublime between the negation of the other into the self and the emptying out of the self into a sea of intertextual echoes. He differs from Church in his ability to embrace what the painter can only suppress. For Church the lesson of intertexuality is a tragic one: It is knowledge of the price that language exacts from us all. Such knowledge comes only at the expense of one's artistic ego. For Ishmael, on the contrary, the otherness of language, its inhuman mockery of originality, is no more than a momentary threat, for what is foreign can still be embraced, and what can be embraced can be redeemed as yet another version of the self. The difference between Church and Ishmael, then, lies in the difference between a sublime that denies the conventionality of its own language and one that affirms it.

We know this from the novel's opening line. "Call me Ishmael" may be read in romantic fashion as a call to creation, an insistence that we create Ishmael by naming him (*"Call* me Ishmael"), for we, like the gods, must bring forth life by an act of the imagination. But our opportunity of creation is also a reminder that we are creatures of convention after all. Our metier – our calling – is naming. Whatever we touch turns, Midas-like, to language. Hence the resonance behind the name Ishmael: It is borrowed property. Ishmael is someone else's name. It makes little difference whether that someone else is an illegitimate son of Abraham or a figment of Melville's imagination. What counts is the borrowing itself, the fact that our identity is *always* borrowed from others. We are not originals; we are figures of language, echoes and renamings of past texts and past cultures. "Call me Ishmael," then, is a double-edged sword. Like the sublime dynamic that it announces, it locates the creation of identity in an act of language, a form of fiction making that knows no boundaries until it knows itself. We do not create *ex nihilo*, but from more ghostly demarcations, turns of language echoing in the mind.

Hence, even before the novel's opening line, we are treated to etymologies and extracts that deny the clarity of a fresh start. *Moby-Dick* does not so much begin with its opening chapter as continue. Melville's achievement in the opening quotations preceding the narrative of *Moby-Dick* is a comic subversion of the convention of novelistic beginnings. We begin not with Ishmael and his tale, but with a disjointed and fragmented series of quotations. Half a century before T. S. Eliot and "The Wasteland," Western civilization lies strewn upon the page in heaps. The feast of culture is over, and all that is left are the bones, the scraps and the remnants, lovingly and cunningly arranged. The lesson of those opening pages is that we, like Ishmael – like all heroes in sublime quest of ourselves – are collage creatures: Our texts, like our egos, are pieces of cultural bric-a-brac sewn happily together. In the

173

beginning was the word, even if it was only that of a "sub-sub-librarian."

Ishmael, then, is not as curious a choice for sublime hero as he might originally appear. His verbal assertiveness represents a mode of sublime discourse that we are accustomed to recognizing. What we are less used to is his silence, that reticence by which he acknowledges the presence of voices other than his own. And yet it is precisely this latter characteristic that renders him a prime candidate for the job. For he personifies not only the older dreams of the egotistical sublime, the attempt from Emerson to Church to render reality a version of the self, but also that second moment in sublime discourse when language takes an inward turn and stumbles upon its own conventions. Ishmael's power lies in his ability to turn that stumble into a soft-shoe: to dance where others fall. By embracing Queequeg, he embraces the mystery of language and affirms his ability to dwell within the margins of his own text.

7

There is an underside to Ishmael's story, a moment when all egotism, mean or otherwise, stumbles upon its linguistic origins and fails to recover. The scene is the famous "Doubloon" chapter, when assorted members of the *Pequod*'s crew stop to gaze at the coin nailed to the ship's mast-head. Each of the novel's central figures reads the Spanish doubloon before him according to his own disposition. Ahab sees in it demonic and narcissistic energies; Starbuck finds in the doubloon the possibilities of a moral imagination; Stubb has to haul out an almanac to interpret it; and Flask reduces it to a piece of currency and wishes that he could spend it.

What interests us about the chapter, however, are not the stereotypical views of the crew that it presents but the sequence of readings that structure the narrative. For we move in this chapter from the sublime (Ahab) to the moral (Starbuck) to the rote and mechanical (Stubbs) to the material and economic (Flask). The "Doubloon" thus follows a reductive pattern, a sequence that we might call anti-idealistic. It reverses the order of Emerson's *Nature*, which began with "Commodity" and advanced to "Idealism" in a progress that mimicked the effort of the individual to dematerialize nature by removing the veil nature places over "higher laws" than its own. Melville's cosmogony, however, concludes not with higher laws but with Pip. His is the last interpretation that we overhear:

> This way comes Pip — poor boy! would he had died, or I; he's half horrible to me. He too has been watching all of these interpreters — myself included — and look now, he comes to read, with that unearthly idiot face. Stand away again and hear him. Hark!"
> "I look, you look, he looks; we look, ye look, they look."
> "Upon my soul, he been studying Murray's Grammar! Improving his mind, poor fellow! But what's that he says now — hist!"
> "I look, you look, he looks; we look, ye look, they look."
> "Why, he's getting it by heart — hist! again."
> "I look, you look, he looks; we look, ye look, they look." (Chap. 99)

Pip is the only observer who does not attempt to interpret the scene before him. He does not try to understand the relation of the three peaks to the valleys and sky of the doubloon. He focuses our attention instead on the interpretive process itself: "I look, you look, he looks; we look, ye look, they look." Pip represents the endpoint of that devolution and regression that haunts all Emersonian idealism. Only he brings us to an end different from what we might have expected. It is not commodity or materialism with which we conclude, but the act of perception itself. Pip gives us the grammar of seeing with no visionary truth, no epiphanies, no egotistical aspirations. He reminds us of what happens to the Emersonian transparent eyeball when it gets trapped by its own rhetoric. For Pip represents a form of seeing with nothing to see but itself.

Emerson had described the problem in "Experience," his essay of 1844 where the light of *Nature* had darkened into a tangible obscure. The sublime heroism of the transparent eyeball hardens into solipsism in the later essay, and the culprit is Emerson's own self-consciousness:

> It is very unhappy, but too late to be helped, the discovery we have made that we exist. That discovery is called the Fall of Man. Ever afterwards we suspect our instruments. We have learned that we do not see directly, but mediately, and that we have no means of correcting these colored and distorting lenses which we are, or of computing the amount of their errors. Perhaps these subject-lenses

have a creative power; perhaps there are no objects. Once we lived in what we saw; now, the rapaciousness of this new power, which threatens to absorb all things, engages us. Nature, art, persons, letters, religions, objects, successively tumble in, and God is but one of its ideas.[6]

The egotistical sublime is brought full circle here. We are not transparent eyeballs so much as "distorting lenses," mechanical "instruments" that can create only by a process of error. The problem is not that we cross out nature in order to rewrite it as a version of ourselves, but that there is no outside upon which to write. We are alone with ourselves, a visionary state so total that it leads the despairing Emerson to proclaim several paragraphs later, "As I am, so I see; use what language we will, we can never say anything but what we are."

Emerson has succeeded too well. He has isolated the seer so completely, voided nature so entirely, that he can observe nothing but the rumblings within his own prose. If we ask what it is that Emerson *fears* in this passage, we discover a rather unexpected answer. It is not the prospect of solipsism, as we might have suspected. *That* comes very close to being the project. What Emerson fears is what we hear suppressed and echoing through his prose. He hints at it – for it is well hidden – in the lines that close the passage:

Do you see that kitten chasing so prettily her own tail? If you could look with her eyes you might see her surrounded with hundreds of figures performing complex dramas, with tragic and comic issues, long conversations, many characters, many ups and downs of fate, – and meantime it is only puss and her tail. How long before our masquerade will end its noise of tambourines, laughter and shouting, and we shall find it was a solitary performance? A subject and an object, – it takes so much to make the galvanic circuit complete, but magnitude adds nothing. What imports it whether it is Kepler and the sphere, Columbus and America, a reader and his book, or puss with her tail?[7]

This is a passage that begins and ends with a cat and her tail, and its project, between its opening and closing images, is to unveil life's "masquerade." It is an exercise more typical of Thoreau than of Emerson, an effort to pare down psychic motion to its most basic economy. As Thoreau descended below "tradition, and delusion, and appearance, that alluvion which covers the globe," so Emerson plunges through "complex dramas" and "conversations" in order to arrive at that single and simple motion that is the visionary self. What he finds is a "galvanic circuit," an image of motion without substance where "magnitude adds nothing." The image is repeated in the structure of his own prose, which begins and ends with puss in pursuit of her tail. It is an image of language, or rather, we might say, of the self as a grammar: a movement of tropes, none of which is significant by itself, along a signifying chain that we may term fate or God, but that finally is nothing but a perennial parade of images.

Emerson is left here not with the solipsistic self – that would be a comfort, for it would still possess "magnitude" – but with Pip's grammar of seeing. The threat posed to the visionary self is that it is a puffery of motion, a conceit and investment woven from the barest of rhetorics. Emerson's fear is that the visionary self reduces to its own language, and all promises of sublime circulation remain fanciful embroideries upon the barest grammar of seeing: "I look, you look, he looks." Pip is like puss with her tail. He is a grammar, the sheer movement of language for its own sake, selfhood reduced to its rhetorical underpinnings.

No wonder Emerson was frightened. The lesson Pip offers, the moral to the story of puss and her tail, is that language is more powerful than the voice that speaks it. Language divides the world into persons and cases ("I look, you look, he looks") at the same time as it reincorporates everything into itself. Vision is only a conceit of words, and the self but a tale within someone else's narrative. "What imports it whether it is Kepler and the sphere, Columbus and America, or puss with her tail?"

Nor is Ishmael finally immune to the tragic force of Emerson's insight. Ishmael succumbs by the end of the novel to the power of the tale that he tells. He survives at last as an "orphan": "And I only am escaped alone to tell thee." *Moby-Dick* concludes with Ishmael displaced from the center of his story to its circumference. He survives not because of that centripetal pull of the ego to incorporate everything into itself, but because he can float "at the margin of the ensuing scene, and in full sight of it." He is saved by the centrifugal tendencies of language to disperse the self into a sea of tales. Ishmael becomes a witness to others' stories. The world he inhabits in the Epilogue is a world denuded of both its narcissistic investments and its egotistical aspirations. The sublime has been reduced from the motions of an omnivorous self to a grammar that reabsorbs all vision into its own circling vortex.

At the end of the story, the "devious cruising *Rachel*" returns to the scene of the *Pequod*'s destruction, searching for "her missing children." She finds no children of her own, but stumbles instead upon Ishmael. *Moby-Dick* thus concludes with an image of displacement. The *Rachel* grafts onto her original mission a new one, as unforeseen as it was inevitable. She comes to bear an unrecognized stranger and his tale. She is a trope finally for the workings of language: for its indirection, its refusal of original purpose, its repetitions of others' stories. Language has become a mode of witness by the end of *Moby-Dick*. It is a medium haunted by drowned men, whose voices are dispersed across a text (or sea) never wholly one's own. In search of our missing children, we discover, like Emerson, that we know ourselves *too* well, for the voice we hear within the whirlwind was only puss with her tail.

NOTES

1. Herman Melville, "Bartleby" (1853), in *Billy Budd, Sailor and Other Stories,* ed. Harold Beaver (Baltimore: Penguin, 1967), pp. 60-1.
2. Melville describes Emerson in a letter to Evert A. Duyckinck, March 3, 1849. After attending a lecture by Emerson, Melville writes, "I love all men who *dive.* Any fish can swim near the surface, but it takes a great whale to go down stairs five miles or more . . ." *The Letters of Herman Melville,* ed. Merrell R. Davis and William H. Gilman (New Haven: Yale University Press, 1960), pp. 78–80.
3. For a discussion of *Kindred Spirits* in an ideological context see the author's "All the World's a Code: Art and Ideology in Nineteenth Century American Painting," *Art Journal,* 44 (1984):328–337. Paintings considered in this paper are discussed at greater length in the author's *Romantic Re-Vision: Culture and Consciousness in Nineteenth Century American Painting and Literature* (Chicago: University of Chicago Press, 1982), pp. 228–36, and "A Grammar of the Sublime, or Intertextuality Triumphant in Turner, Cole and Church," *New Literary History* 16 (1984–85):321–41.

4. Ralph Waldo Emerson, "Nature" (1836) in Stephen E. Whicher, ed., *Selections from Ralph Waldo Emerson* (Boston: Houghton Mifflin, 1957), p. 24.
5. Henry David Thoreau, *Walden* (1854) in *Walden and Other Writings*, ed. Brooks Atkinson (New York: Modern Library, 1950), p. 73.
6. Emerson, *Selections*, p. 269.
7. Ibid., p. 271.

Notes on Contributors

Richard H. Brodhead, editor of this volume, is Professor of English at Yale University. His works include *Hawthorne, Melville, and the Novel* and *The School of Hawthorne,* as well as the collection *Faulkner: New Perspectives.*

Lawrence Buell is Professor of English and Chair of the Department of English at Oberlin College. Author of *Literary Transcendentalism* and *New England Literary Culture: From Revolution through Renaissance,* he has also coedited *The Morgesons and Other Writings* by Elizabeth Stoddard.

T. Walter Herbert, Jr., is Herman Brown Professor of English and University Scholar at Southwestern University. He is the author of *Moby-Dick and Calvinism: A World Dismantled* and *Marquesan Encounters: Melville and the Meaning of Civilization.*

James McIntosh is Associate Professor of English and Director of the American Culture Program at the University of Michigan. He is the author of *Thoreau as Romantic Naturalist* and essays on Emerson, Melville, Goethe, and Hawthorne and has edited the Norton Critical Edition of *Nathaniel Hawthorne's Tales.*

Carolyn Porter is Associate Professor of English at the University of California, Berkeley. She has written *Seeing and Being: The Plight of the Participant Observer in Emerson, James, Adams, and Faulkner* and is at work on a book on Melville.

Bryan Wolf, Associate Professor of English and American Studies and Director of Graduate Studies in the American Studies Program at Yale, is the author of *Romantic Re-vision: Culture and Consciousness in Nineteenth-Century American Painting and Literature* and several other essays on literary and visual texts.

Selected Bibliography

Throughout this volume, *Moby-Dick* is cited from the Library of America edition (New York, 1984), which uses the authoritative text established by Harrison Hayford, Hershel Parker, and G. Thomas Tanselle for the Northwestern-Newberry Edition of the Writings of Herman Melville. For the convenience of readers who have other editions, quotations are followed by chapter numbers in *Moby-Dick*.

Readers interested in other works by Melville will find his complete prose works collected in three Library of America volumes prepared by G. Thomas Tanselle and Harrison Hayford. The standard biography is Leon Howard's *Herman Melville, a Biography* (Berkeley and Los Angeles: University of California Press, 1967), which is valuably supplemented by Jay Leyda's two-volume *The Melville Log: A Documentary Life of Herman Melville, 1819–1891* (New York: Gordian Press, 1969). For quite different psychological and political readings of Melville's life, see also Edwin Haviland Miller, *Melville* (New York: Braziller, 1975), and Michael Paul Rogin, *Subversive Genealogy*, cited in the following list. Criticism of *Moby-Dick* is voluminous. Two still useful collections of Melville criticism are Richard Chase's *Melville: A Collection of Critical Essays* (Englewood Cliffs, N.J.: Prentice-Hall, 1962) and Hershel Parker and Harrison Hayford's *Moby-Dick as Doubloon* (New York: Norton, 1970). In addition some of the more important critical studies are cited in the list that follows:

Berthoff, Warner. *The Example of Melville*. Princeton, N.J.: Princeton University Press, 1962.

Brodhead, Richard H. *Hawthorne, Melville, and the Novel*. Chicago: University of Chicago Press, 1976.

Brodtkorb, Paul, Jr. *Ishmael's White World*. New Haven, Conn.: Yale University Press, 1965.

Cameron, Sharon. *The Corporeal Self: Allegories of the Body in Melville and Hawthorne*. Baltimore: Johns Hopkins University Press, 1981.

Caserio, Robert L. *Plot, Story, and the Novel*. Princeton, N.J.: Princeton University Press, 1979.

Charvat, William. *The Profession of Authorship in America, 1800–1870.* Columbus: Ohio State University Press, 1968.

Douglas, Ann. *The Feminization of American Culture.* New York: Alfred A. Knopf, 1977.

Dryden, Edgar A. *Melville's Thematics of Form.* Baltimore: Johns Hopkins University Press, 1968.

Feidelson, Charles. *Symbolism and American Literature.* Chicago: University of Chicago Press, 1953.

Herbert, T. Walter, Jr. *Moby-Dick and Calvinism.* New Brunswick, N.J.: Rutgers University Press, 1977.

Irwin, John T. *American Hieroglyphics.* Baltimore: Johns Hopkins University Press, 1980.

Lawrence, D. H. *Studies in Classic American Literature* (1923). Reprinted New York: Viking Press, 1964.

Matthiessen, F. O. *American Renaissance.* New York: Oxford University Press, 1941.

Milder, Robert. "The Composition of *Moby-Dick:* A Review and a Prospect." *Emerson Society Quarterly* 23 (1977):203–16.

Olson, Charles. *Call Me Ishmael.* San Francisco: City Lights, 1947.

Pease, Donald E. "*Moby-Dick* and the Cold War." In Walter Benn Michaels and Donald E. Pease, eds., *The American Renaissance Reconsidered.* Baltimore: Johns Hopkins University Press, 1985.

Richardson, Robert D., Jr. *Myth and Literature in the American Renaissance.* Bloomington: Indiana University Press, 1978.

Rogin, Michael Paul. *Subversive Genealogy : The Politics and Art of Herman Melville.* New York: Alfred A. Knopf, 1983.

Simpson, David. *Fetishism and Imagination.* Baltimore: Johns Hopkins University Press, 1982.

Smith, Henry Nash. *Democracy and the Novel.* New York: Oxford University Press, 1978.

Wadlington, Warwick. *The Confidence Game in American Literature.* Princeton, N.J.: Princeton University Press, 1975.

Ziff, Larzer. *Literary Democracy: The Declaration of Cultural Independence in America.* New York: Viking Press, 1981.

Zoeller, Robert. *The Salt-Sea Mastodon: A Reading of Moby-Dick.* Berkeley and Los Angeles: University of California Press, 1973.